DEAR READER,

I HOPE YOU FIND SOME

SENSE IN THIS — & A

FEW LAUGHS!

Jacob Boswell

D1340200

ROTCHESTER
1.2.13

# SENSE AND NONSENSE

Conversations with a clown about spiritual things

## *Malcolm Rothwell*

authorHOUSE®

*AuthorHouse™ UK Ltd.*
*500 Avebury Boulevard*
*Central Milton Keynes, MK9 2BE*
*www.authorhouse.co.uk*
*Phone: 08001974150*

*First published by AuthorHouse 2/28/2011*

*ISBN: 978-1-4567-7010-5*

*The hymn 'when we are tempted in our pride' by Elizabeth*
*Cosnett is printed by permission of Stainer and Bell Ltd.*

*'Tea in the desert' is printed by permission of Edwina Gately.*

*The meditation 'O God, the source of common life'*
*is printed by permission of Christian Aid.*

*The poem 'God and coffee' is by Hilaire Kirkland, a New*
*Zealand poet who died in the1970s. Unfortunately, I have*
*been unable to find the original source of this poem.*

*All biblical references are taken from the New Revised*
*Standard Version (OUP 1995) unless otherwise stated.*

*This book is printed on acid-free paper.*

This book is dedicated to the family
of Lucy and Malcolm and
their partners:
the next generation:

Louise and Brendan
Larry and Lisa
Oliver and Rachel
Mandie and Scarlet
Phil and Louise

# Contents

# ACKNOWLEDGEMENTS

I am indebted to a number of people:-

my lovely wife Lucy, for taking the time to read the original script and for all her valuable insights, patience and encouragement.

my friend, the Revd. Brenda Woods, for her careful and patient reading of the manuscript. She gave many insightful and creative suggestions as well as correcting my grammar.

Leslie Griffiths for his kind comments which finally persuaded me that the book was worth publishing.

My step daughter, Mandie, for the original idea behind the front cover.

my friend Helen Hays for telling me about the poem by Hilaire Kirkland.

finally, to our family for all the fun and laughter that they provide, not to mention the grandchildren they have produced! Georgia, Macie, Jake, Hannah, Sophie and Isabella.

# PREFACE

I said yes, I'd endorse this book. After all, the author is a friend. However, I am a busy man so I thought I would just skim through it and write a nice, if anodyne, sentence or two; to show willing. That, after all, is what friends do.

It didn't turn out that way. This book took hold of me and would not let me go until I had finished it. The format, the content, the pungency and the passion quite overwhelmed me.

This is a first-rate work of apologetics with no cant, no obfuscation, a sustained focus and lots of energy. It is a must, not only for old stagers like me, but for anyone else who wants to get inside the meaning of faith without the trappings or the entanglements of a previous age.

I found it immensely pleasurable and I can only hope it gets a wide readership.

> The Revd the Lord Griffiths of Burry Port
> Minister of Wesley's Chapel, London
> Former President of the Methodist Conference

# Introduction

This book is written for all who feel they are on a journey and are searching for something good and lasting. It is written for people who may be in the church, or hanging on by their finger nails, or for those who have long since found the church to be an irrelevance. It is written for those who are questioning their faith because of the challenges thrown up by the culture we live in and takes the form of a conversation between myself and a clown called Zeno. If I lapse into technical words then Zeno challenges me to explain myself. In fact, Zeno comes from the court jester tradition where questions are asked that nobody else dare ask. He, therefore, forces me to be honest and not hide behind jargon, or a barrage of long words and long sentences.

Zeno also stops me getting too serious and constantly brings me down to earth. I am sure we could do with a little more humour in our lives and in the church. We take ourselves far too seriously. All you have to do is look at any function where church dignitaries are present. It is like a fancy dress parade but everybody is so serious. Symbols and vestments are used long after their former meaning has been forgotten. Anyway, who was it who said, laughter is the best medicine? I am sure there is something deeply moving and deeply spiritual about a good laugh.

This book is a light hearted attempt to steer a course through some of the issues affecting those who are trying to live a

Christian or spiritual life today. Much of the material is drawn from my own experience as a Methodist Minister. What has happened to the church in this secular age? How has scientific progress affected faith? What are the difficulties associated with prayer? Are we all being sucked into leading evermore busy lives rather than spending time just being? Is there a danger that people can be lulled into an escapist mentality? What is spirituality? Am I as free as I think I am? How do I choose among the many choices I am presented with each day? What will happen to the church?

Each chapter closes with some questions to ponder and something to aid meditation. Although there is a thread going through the book each chapter can be read as an independent unit.

Some readers will find what I have written to be a great challenge and a bit disconcerting. Others will be comforted to think they are not alone on their spiritual journey. This is at one and the same time the challenge of the Christian faith. One can find words of great comfort, for example, in the Bible, but at the same time, and probably on the same page, there are words which take you out of your comfort zone.

I very much hope that you will enjoy reading this book as much as I have enjoyed writing it. Hopefully, you will have a good laugh from time to time but also see that important issues are being wrestled with.

# Chapter One

## THE BIRTH OF A CLOWN

My name is Zeno. I know that is a strange name but I do have a very unconventional background. In actual fact I am only twenty years old and I came into being not through natural parents but in a most unusual way. Let me explain.

My other self is a minister of religion, a Methodist minister to be precise although he argues that denominations are a thing of the past, about as relevant as dinosaurs, extinct. That is as maybe. Who am I to argue? Anyway, as I was saying twenty years ago, maybe it was a bit more, or a bit less, does it matter? - he went to a conference. This was a place where other ministers had gathered to talk about their work. It is a funny kind of work and nobody seems to know what they do except on Sundays and that can be a terrible bore. How can Good News be so boring? Sometimes I hear a good joke and the first thing I want to do is tell somebody. 'Did you hear the one about……?' That's my job, spreading happiness and laughter. I once heard it said that laughter is like internal jogging. Don't forget that laughter is also the shortest distance between two people. What is required is a bit more fun and enjoyment on Sunday mornings. Now where was I?

1

These ministers had gathered together for a conference entitled 'circus'. That sounds a little bit odd even to me but when you think about it, and you don't have to think very hard, there was something interesting going on. Certainly there is the general understanding that circus folk generally look after each other. They live close to each other and are mutually supportive. Circus folk are often referred to as a family. Then there are the various acts. For example, circus usually involves a juggling act and there are many people who in their everyday lives struggle to keep various balls in the air or plates whirling round the end of sticks scared to death lest one of them should fall to the ground. Then there are those who are completely stressed out because they feel they are walking on a tight rope and the slightest movement will leave them plunging, metaphorically, to their death. The stress can be because they fear for their job, or their inability to pay the mortgage, or the fact they would like to marry and cannot find a partner, or they fear that their offspring will make some wrong choices, or there is a fear of contracting the dreaded cancer, or they will be found out because of an illicit relationship. The list is endless.

Somewhere in between the more hair raising and dexterous acts come the clowns. For some reasons clowns can scare people but this is not their object in life. Quite the reverse. There is a very good film starring Robin Williams who was training to be a doctor but he gets so fed up with the stiff and starchy approach he found in hospitals that he started to go into the wards dressed as a clown. His objective was to bring fun back into people's lives, even if they were dying. He tried to grant them their favourite fantasy such has having a bath full of chocolate surrounded by big balloons. What a wonderful image! Perhaps not surprisingly Patch Adams, that was the doctor's name, was castigated by the authorities of the medical school. How could he be so silly? Medicine is a serious business. People have to be treated very seriously. This is no laughing matter. Adams went on to found his own hospital in America which had a much more relaxed attitude to health care and an approach that was perceived to be in the patient's best interests.

I know that my other personality, M, always start to get worried when people know what is good for other people. He says Christians are very good at that. They know what Mr.Bloggs needs and they pray to God that she will give it to him. (I know I am also implying here that God is female but there are female images of God in the bible.) People have the audacity to tell God how to conduct his business! Surely the only people who know what is best for them are the individuals themselves. There is the famous occasion when Jesus asks the blind man, 'What do you want me to do for you?' Of course, we all know don't we? He wants to see again so how stupid of Jesus to ask him. It is so obvious. Jesus has the uncanny knack of not taking away a person's integrity but always giving them the right to choose for themselves. I like that. The choice is with me. I don't feel bludgeoned, cajoled, manipulated, driven or controlled. Jesus invites and I choose.

Talking of choice, M told me that he had to choose at the conference which workshop to attend. Was he going to learn more about juggling, tightrope walking or clowning and how these various skills related to everyday life? He was very much attracted to the first one and indeed, even now tries to juggle a bit, but his gut reaction was to go for the latter. I have since learned in talking with him that his interest in clowns goes back a long way. Indeed, he has often wrestled with and preached about what Paul writes about in his letter to the Corinthians. Paul writes there in chapter one that the wisdom of the world counts for very little. God has made the wisdom of the world foolish. What is important is the foolishness of God and the folly of the cross which is much wiser than human wisdom. That turns human ideas upside down straightaway – or are they turned the right way up? God chooses what is foolish in the world to shame the wise and what is weak to shame the strong. Anyway it was in the clown workshop that I started to come alive. M has told me in some detail how it all came to pass.

He dutifully attended workshops on clowning and very good they were too. There were lots of ideas about trusting each other; finding the clown within ourselves, finding out particular ways of walking because all clowns have a different walk, and how to apply makeup or slap as it is called in the trade. The problem with M was that although he knew about clowns in his head he had never dreamt of actually being a clown and so when the workshop became more hands on he really struggled. M wanted to know about clowns but certainly not be one. Dressing up and putting on a stupid face was not for him. Oh dear me no. That was taking things a bit too far. It is all very well to agree to something and even to preach about it but to actually put the words into practice is quite a different kettle of fish. My uneducated guess is that is precisely where a lot of you struggle. Who was it who said that Christianity has been tried and found wanting but the reply came back, it has never been tried because it has been found too difficult.

To cut a long story short, foolishness prevailed and M decided to put on a face. That is where the trouble began. What face could he put on? There are basically two kinds of clown. There is the white faced clown and the Auguste clown. The former is the straight character to the latter's pranks and jokes. These are familiar figures to any one who has visited a circus. M attempted to become an Auguste clown but some how it did not feel right. The group actually dressed up in clown clothes and visited a local hostelry. Even though they looked odd and very out of the ordinary, no one paid them any attention. Were they too threatening or were people too embarrassed? Who knows? I sometimes observe that a dog collar can evoke similar reactions.

On returning from this night on the town M began to ponder and express his discomfort. The root of the problem lay with a certain amount of facial hair. Auguste clowns do not have beards. Who would have thought that a little bit of hair could cause so much trouble. However, all was not lost. The group leader mentioned the fact that there was another kind of clown, especially in the USA. This was the hobo or tramp clown. M felt a burden had been lifted. Deep within his soul something had stirred. He knew who he was after many years of searching. Not that he could put a particular name to this new found identity. He just knew and that is a good place to be. A face, my face, began to emerge. I began to take form and shape and have a life even if not a name. As you see mine was no ordinary birth. There were lots of other people around and the midwife was a professional clown who was superb in offering words of encouragement just at the right time.

The conference was drawing to a close and the last act was about to take place. In traditional form the participants had decided to close with a Eucharistic service. Nothing unusual in that except this time people had to bring something of their workshop experience into the service. This is where I made my first public appearance! I was very nervous to say the least, and not at all well dressed for the occasion. M had given me an old rag bag of clothes to wear and my face left a lot to be desired. Like all newborns I was a sight to behold and one could only guess what the finished product, the adult version, would look like.

I have to say that the service was very traditional and not something my forbears would have tolerated. Can you imagine those early 'fools for Christ' being so miserable as they celebrated the Risen Lord? For them every gathering together was a thanksgiving and a celebration. Furthermore, being dressed as I was, I actually felt very much an outsider and wondered whether I was entitled to bread and wine. That is an odd thought. Didn't Jesus spend much of his ministry bringing in those who were on the outside, the leper, the prostitute and the tax collector, not to mention women and children? People who had no status were so esteemed that Jesus often had a meal with them. That is a wonderful albeit it, costly, way of supporting and loving people in a very practical way. The thought also occurred to me that it was very odd of the people behind the table to consume between them the remains of the bread and wine. Circus life is about supporting each other, the strong supporting the weak, the rich the poorer and so on. Can it be right that some eat too much whilst others grow hungry? What message is being declared in these actions?

I began to get very disconcerted and the final hymn was the last straw. It was sung like a dirge and so I, on the spur of the moment, took my hat off and pretended to take a collection. Going round the congregation in this way at least and at last brought a smile to some faces. But it felt like hard work. The important thing was, though, I had seen the light of day. I had come to life after many years secret gestation. M had struggled with the birth pains but eventually he had given in. There is no doubt it was difficult getting used to having me around. One's life is never the same again after giving birth. Unfortunately, at this stage I still did not have a name.

On the way back from the conference M was in deep thought about all that had happened and the internal changes that had taken place. These were not exactly seismic but they were very significant and life changing. On nearing his manse M happened to pass by a church on the steps of which was sitting a genuine person of the road. M spoke to him. He had quite a posh accent and was, under the circumstances, well dressed. To M's amazement and quiet amusement, this gentleman also had a telephone. This was a phone of the type one plugged into the wall. Mobiles were not yet common place. Can you imagine the scene? This tramp, living rough on the streets of London, was trying to dress as a gentleman and possess some of the trappings of a gentleman? Since that time M has allowed me to have my own phone and surprise, surprise, mysteriously it works without being plugged in. More importantly I was given the name Zeno. In a flash of inspiration, one could hardly say genius, M remembered that Zeno was well known for paradoxes and here was a paradox before his very eyes. I became the gentleman tramp clown known as Zeno.

Of course, all philosophers will have heard of Zeno but some of you may not. He was born round about 490BC in Elea, Lucanian, now southern Italy, and died in the same place about 425BC. Very little of his life is known except that he was a philosopher who became famous because of his paradoxes. The most famous of these is about Achilles running a race with a tortoise. Now my money would be on Achilles to win the race. Indeed it would be on anybody winning a race against a tortoise, but Zeno, being very wise, gave a different solution.

Achilles is so confident of victory he gives the tortoise a head start. Zeno supposedly proves that Achilles can never overtake the tortoise. Here is his argument. Before Achilles can overtake the tortoise, he must first run to point A, where the tortoise started. But then the tortoise has crawled to point B. Now Achilles must run to point B. But the tortoise has gone to point C, etc. Achilles is stuck in a situation in which he gets closer and closer to the tortoise, but never catches him.

This might sound very wise but it is all very confusing to me. At least I know why I have been called Zeno. I much prefer another little-known story. Achilles didn't win the above race. So, he challenged the tortoise to a pole vault competition, double or nothing. The tortoise's pole bent impressively, before it catapulted him out of Greece, never to be seen again.

My second public appearance was in a central London church. Of course, my appearance had taken on more respectability in the meantime. I now had a decent bowler hat, a reasonably smart pin stripe suit although it had seen better days and a red nose as befitted my character. I have had to endure all kinds of noses but I am comfortable with my present one. My face is in keeping with my identity and I am more or less happy with it although sometimes I wish I could make some changes here and there. Who doesn't? But cosmetic surgery seems very drastic and usually a complete waste of money. Part of the secret it seems to me is to maximise what we have been given rather than be so discontented with it. We have to play with the cards that we have been dealt rather than for ever moaning that our cards are not very good. I have to say I am not really given to poetry except limericks of course, but recently I came across something that I found quite startling. It is a poem by Ann Lewin in which she recalls that Jesus turned water into wine but bemoans the fact that 'being faithless, we turn the wine of our potential to plain water'. (1) As ever I am getting sidetracked.

There is no doubt that going into the Sunday worship of a typical congregation for the first time is not an easy thing to do at the best of times but it is even more difficult when you are dressed as I was. I had no idea how the people would react. My feelings were very deep and very strong. After all I had never been in a church before. I had no idea what to do. Where should I sit? Would people speak to me? I felt very isolated and vulnerable because I was dressed differently to everybody else. They kept looking at me. Had I done something wrong? I tried very hard to fit in with them and do what they were doing but sometimes I stood up at the wrong time and then sat down at the wrong time. I just felt very uncomfortable. Everything seemed so strange. The music was unfamiliar and I am not used to having so many books in my hands. It is all so difficult when everybody else seems to know what they are doing and nobody gives you any help. For some strange reason they all seemed so embarrassed and kept avoiding my glances. As for people coming round asking for money, that was the end. I didn't have any. I had to search around and for the sake of appearances put an old button in the bag. Hopefully, no one saw it. This was not my style, much too stiff and starchy for someone like me. Again, I began to ponder how Jesus would feel today if he entered a church service. Would he feel at ease or feel uncomfortable? Would he feel excluded or welcomed? For sure, sometimes the acts of worship I have attended come across as pure theatre with the main participants being in fancy dress and the congregation passively watching like a theatre audience. I do feel there is more involvement at a circus. The audience are often on the edge of their seats and I am able to wander around talking and laughing with some of them. Sometimes we bring them into the arena and we all enjoy ourselves.

Going back to the service I walked into, I was again struck with a very deep feeling when the bread and wine was served to me. Was it acceptable for me to have some? If so could I have a bit more please? Such a small piece of bread and such a small sip of wine and I was feeling so hungry and thirsty. I was absolutely delighted to go to one service where the bread for communion was a large loaf. It looked very impressive and reminded me of the generosity of God. Yes, I know, Holy Communion is not supposed to be a full-scale meal, more a spiritual nourishment, but I bet those early Christians had a good time at least. They were celebrating. These days, everybody seems afraid to be themselves as though some of their humanity has been left on the church steps. I thought Christianity was to enable us to become more human and more whole. Have Christians lost their true identity behind a façade of piety?

Talking of identity, let me tell you about some of my ancestors. They were called court jesters. These people had the wonderful capacity, almost literally, to get away with murder, as they told the sovereign of the day some home truths that other people were scared to articulate. They got away with it because of the humour that they dressed their words in. Court jesters tended not to be taken too seriously but their words contained notes of caution. Of course I could go even farther tracing my lineage back to some Old Testament prophets. Do you remember, for example, Isaiah, going round stripped and barefoot for three years as a sign and portent against Egypt (Isaiah chapter 20). What a 'foolish' thing to do!! Of course, the example par excellence, of foolish behaviour which makes a point is that of Jesus. As M tells me who but a clown would ride into Jerusalem on a donkey, or turn water into a huge amount of wine, or tell oppressed people to go the extra mile with their captors, and turn the other cheek when struck by their enemy, and pray for their enemies. It is odd to say the least when the last will be first and in order to find yourself you have to lose yourself. I ask you, have you ever tried to lose something?! What about a camel going through the eye of a needle? Why, it would get stuck at the first hump! Who but a clown would perform the extraordinary feat of rising from the dead? Jesus was not the 'fitting household pet for pale curates and pious old ladies' that Dorothy L. Sayers once declared we had made him. (2)

That reminds me of another of my public appearances. They are few and far between these days. I was allowed to put on a short act during an Easter morning service. On that day of the year it seems to be that almost anything is possible but I can assure you the last thing the assembled folk expected to see was a clown. However, we had a lot of fun trying to blow balloons up. It never ceases to amaze me how laughter can bring people together and unite them. Where before there had been a cold formality, now there was a more relaxed atmosphere. There was more than a hint of celebration in the air. 'Good Christians all rejoice and sing' was sung with great gusto. (3) From my point of view it was as though the shell of an egg had been broken. Instead of staying with the sad, painful and miserable feelings of Good Friday new life began to emerge. I cashed in on this and did a little stunt of putting a long pin into a balloon without bursting it. This is not magic, it can be done. I then tried to persuade the congregation to go home and tell their friends what had happened. They had seen a real life clown in their church service and he had put a pin in a balloon without it bursting. Would they believe it? Presumably 'some doubted'. (Matt 28:17) There is always a danger of trying to find out how things are done rather than simply enjoying the experience.

So you see, I have a long and illustrious line of ancestors. It is continued today by people like Roly Bain, who have a clown ministry. They belong to a group called Holy Fools. These are people who have not been afraid to show their vulnerability in the interests of disclosing a profound truth. Many is the time that they have been simply laughed at or ignored but sometimes, as in the life of Jesus, they have provoked such extraordinary anger that they have been exterminated. Such is the power of a clown's antics. I find it all rather scary but then I think that M finds the Christian life a scary challenge. There are those well- known injunctions in the New Testament to take up one's cross to follow Jesus. Looking at it from the outside as I do it seems to me that not many people have forsaken much, let alone their lives to follow Jesus. In many ways the life style of a Christian seems very similar to the life style of a non- believer. I wonder what it is that makes a Christian different? Is it simply because they go to church, sometimes read the bible and sometimes pray or is it something more profound and basic than that? Isn't there something in the bible about salt and yeast? If salt is to be of any use at all then it must retain its saltiness. In the same way yeast has to be fresh and not stale. Doesn't Jesus invite his followers to be like 'salt' and 'yeast'?

M likes to draw a distinction between being a Christian and being Christian. The former, he says, is simply a term that distinguishes a person from being, say, a Muslim or a Jew, but the latter, being an adjective is much more descriptive. How Christian are you? How Christ like are you? To be truly Christian one needs to be far more than a nominal Christian. I don't think that is easy. I find it hard enough being a clown with some juggling thrown in. Some people are natural but most of us need hours and hours of practice. Indeed, it would be impossible for me without help, advice, support and discipline. Indeed, the support and friendship of like minded souls is vital. You must know that the best comedians look as though they have made their act up on the spot but the reality is that it has taken hours of practice to refine their art and their timing.

The other day I was talking to M about prayer. It baffles me that some people think prayer is easy and all you have to do is utter some words to God and he will then do his bit. Surely for prayer to be effective there has to be a sense of working at prayer. M agreed with me. He said that if we are to discern God's will for us then this will take time and effort. Supremely, time is needed to listen to God otherwise we are like the patient who tells the doctor all about his aches and pains but doesn't wait for the doctor's diagnosis or prescription. We can listen to God in a variety of ways; simply by being quiet; by reading a passage of the bible and asking what it has to say to us, today; by reviewing our own experience and asking where God is in it; and by looking at what is happening in the world, church or world and asking what God is saying through those facts. I think it is all too easy to think we know what God wants but he is always full of surprises.

One day three men were walking along and came upon a raging, violent river. They needed to get to the other side. The first man prayed to God saying: "Please God, give me the strength to cross this river." Poof, God gave him big arms and strong legs and he was able to swim across the river in about two hours. Seeing this, the second man prayed to God saying, "Please God, give me the strength and the ability to cross this river." Poof, God gave him a rowing boat and he was able to row across the river in about three hours. The third man had seen how this worked out for the other two, so he also prayed to God saying: "Please God, give me the strength, ability and intelligence to cross this river." Poof, God turned him into a woman. She looked at the map and walked across the bridge.

Whee-eeeee!!!! The God of surprises has done it again. He keeps doing things and saying things that we don't expect. We don't always see the funny side so it is a good job that God has a sense a humour. My main job as Zeno is not to analyse but to make people laugh. I leave that to other people and sometimes even to M in his better moments. Laughter is a vital part of my life. If I am not making people laugh I can hardly be called a clown. That is the sole reason for my existence. Of course some people take offence at this approach. These are the people who like to argue and score debating points to show how clever they are. M is cleverer than I am and he tells me that during the time of St. Paul these were the Greeks. They enjoyed the cut and thrust of debate and followed up with clever philosophical arguments. Paul says that they were 'offended' by Christianity. On the other hand there are those who want a clear sign from heaven that Christianity is true and that God does exist. At the time of Paul these were the Jews and they longed for a miracle because otherwise they found the message of Christianity 'nonsense'.

These groups of people still exist today although we might

give them different names. There are those who live in the world of ideas and derive great pleasure from doing so. From what I have observed this is mainly a male phenomenon. They like to know where they stand and not be doing with anything that appears to be plain stupid. Of course there are others who simply like to know for sure that certain things are indisputably true. That however, would not be the life of faith. M agrees with this entirely. He says the life of faith by definition is not the life of sight and therefore not the life of absolute certainty. That feeling, which some have called assurance, comes from a different place than in the head. It is those parts I try to reach and which I think Jesus reached. Why else would people have given up everything and decided to follow him? He spoke to their inner need. He quenched their spiritual thirst and longing. He gave them hope for the future. Their lives began to have meaning and purpose. For some reason people were prepared even to die for him.

However, I seem to have digressed yet again. It is part of my nature. I know that one of the things that attracts M to Christianity is its corporate nature. He says it would have been impossible for the early Christians to think of being a Christian on one's own. Indeed, from a New Testament point of view the thought of being a Christian in isolation from other Christians would have been a contradiction in terms. He says that Paul, when writing about the church, used corporate metaphors like the vine or the body or the household of God. If you want to be a Christian on your own then think about a piece of coal which when taken from a burning fire soon loses its warmth and potency. Likewise, a banana, when it leaves the bunch soon gets skinned.

From my point of view it would be impossible to be a one-man circus. No one person would be capable of performing all the acts in a typical circus. So if we follow Paul's example of the body, no one Christian can exhibit all the gifts of the Christian Body. Indeed, if a foot, for example, is cut off from the rest of the body it is undoubtedly still a foot but it can no longer function as a foot. I wonder why it is that some people insist that they can be a Christian without going to church. The assumption must be that Christianity is just a matter of common sense and therefore anyone can be a Christian. On the other hand many are probably bored with the whole church phenomenon and who can blame them?

I know for a fact that Jesus invited people to follow him, to experience life of a new and lasting quality, to experience deeper relationships with each other, to experience a life of wholeness, to enjoy life in all its wonder and abundance, to get a deeper understanding of God. What could be more exciting than that? Woe to those who ever contrive to make such good news boring. Sometimes M does!!

Now I am not clever enough to write a whole book unless it was a joke book, so I'm going to let Malcolm take over. I will, however, have my say from time to time and keep him on his toes.

## Points to ponder:

1. How do you feel about laughing in church?

2. Is there a clown in you waiting to escape? What kind of clown would you be?
   Can you draw your face? Do you have a name?
   What kind of walk would you have?

3. Which parts of the New Testament, if any, do you find foolish?

4. When was the last time you did anything foolish for God ? or anything foolish at all?

5. What do you make of the verse 'For God's foolishness is wiser than human wisdom, and God's weakness is stronger than human strength'? (1 Cor. 1:25)

## Meditation:

> When we are tempted in our pride
> To dizzy heights of sin,
> Beneath our feet, O Lord, provide
> A ripe banana skin,
> And when we yearn at someone's head
> To let a brickbat fly,
> Give us the grace to use instead
> A well-aimed custard pie.
>
> When cherished institutions stand
> Before your throne of grace,
> With good intentions in each hand
> And egg on every face,
> Teach us to query grand designs
> With laughter born of tears,
> For deep in earth's jam-butty mines
> Your rainbow still appears.
>
> Along with zeal to do your will
> We ask a sense of fun,
> A touch of sugar on the pill,

A currant in the bun.
Like him who saw a desert bush
With Heaven's glory crowned,
May we through the incongruous
Discover holy ground. (4)

# References

1. Lewin, Ann, <u>Watching for the Kingfisher,</u> Inspire, 2004, p.17
2. see Morgan, Alison, <u>The Wild Gospel</u>, Monarch Books, 2005, p.62
3. Hymns and Psalms, 191
4. Hymn by Elizabeth Cosnett in <u>Hymns for Everyday Saints</u>, Stainer and Bell, Ltd.

# Chapter 2

## SCIENCE AND BIBLICAL TRUTH

A major challenge to belief in the existence of God has come from science. One of the early challenges to the biblical explanation of the beginning of the world and its place in the universe was made by Galileo in the early part of the seventeenth century in Padua, Italy. Building on the work of the astronomer, Copernicus, Galileo dared to suggest that the earth was not static and, was not the centre of the universe. Moreover, it was not flat but round.

Z: That was a big thing to say because it seems to me that the earth is static. If it is moving, how come everything doesn't fall off?

We'll come to that in a minute. Instead of everything revolving round the earth, Galileo said that everything revolved around the sun. At the time, this was regarded as nothing short of heresy and contrary to biblical teaching. In one place it is asserted that Joshua ordered the sun and moon to stand still (Joshua 10:12). This being the case, clearly the implication was that the earth was static and all heavenly bodies moved around it. Not only that, the bible is quite clear in its depiction of God as creator of the earth and this clearly implies that the earth is the centre of all the universe. Indeed, how could it be anything else because when the creation stories were compiled little was known of anything outside the seen world. The known world was very, very small and must have seemed like the centre of everything. The biblical world view was shaken to its roots by the work of Galileo.

Z: I must admit I've always thought of heaven as being somewhere up above the clouds but I guess we don't need scientists to tell us that can't be true. All we need is a few space travellers to say they have not seen heaven on their travels.

That's right and with regards to why we don't fall off the earth that was explained by someone called Isaac Newton who came along about a hundred years after Galileo and worked out his three laws of motion that established the framework for modern physics and also explained the movement of the planets. It is said that as a result of watching an apple fall to the ground he developed his theory of gravity.

Z: An unlikely tale if ever I heard one!

As a result of these laws Newton was able to assert that the universe behaved in entirely predictable ways, that is, according to certain fixed laws. The problem for students of the bible is that those laws often appear to be broken. To mention just a few examples: Moses heard the voice of God in a burning bush that was not consumed (Exodus 3: 1-6); Moses sent Aaron to Pharoah to plead for freedom with a staff that could turn into a snake (Exodus 7: 9); on Mount Carmel, Elijah called down fire from heaven to consume an offering that had been drenched with water three times thereby discrediting the prophets of Baal and giving God the glory (1 Kings 18: 20-30); when the iron head of an axe head fell into the water Elisha made it float so that it could be recovered (2 Kings 6: 1-7); and the prophet Jonah is said to have lived in the belly of a big fish for three days and three nights (Jonah 3:17).

Z: A very fishy tale, but it reminds me of another story. A teacher was telling her class that it was physically impossible for a whale to swallow a human because its throat was very small. However, a little girl in the class insisted that Jonah had indeed been swallowed by a whale. The teacher became very irritated and repeated that it was physically impossible. The little girl said, "When I get to heaven I will ask Jonah". The teacher asked, "What if Jonah went to hell?" As quick as a flash the little girl retorted, "Then you ask him".

I think we had better move on to the New Testament where there are many more examples. Jesus raised a widows son from death (Luke 7: 11—15 ) as indeed Elijah had done hundreds of years earlier (1 Kings 17: 15-24); he calmed the storm ( Luke 8: 22-25);he walked on water (Matt.14: 25-27); he raised Lazarus from the dead (John 11: 1-43) and, of course, he himself is raised from the dead. What are we to make of all these apparent contradictions to Newtonian law? Can we simply say that God intervenes at will to contravene these laws?

Z: I'm beginning to get very confused! Are you trying to tell me that some events in the bible didn't happen because God didn't intervene in the way we thought?

If God intervened, wouldn't that make for a very unreliable universe? Perhaps it is time to ask other questions. Instead of the question 'did it really happen?' a more fruitful line of approach would be 'what does it mean?' or 'what is the significance of this event?' In particular, what does it mean for living today in the twenty first century?

Z: Is it any good asking whether the resurrection happened?

You can ask the question but there are differing answers. All we can say for sure is that something happened!!

Z: I often wondered what Jesus wore when he rose from the grave!

There you go again. It is not a helpful question. The whole point is that lives were transformed when people realised that Jesus was alive in them. That is the relevance for us today. Instead of leading fearful, closed up, stunted lives we can live life to the full.

Z: I'm beginning to get the idea – I think! But can you give me another example because I'm a little bit slow on the uptake.

Well let's take the feeding of the five thousand.

Z: Where would you want to take five thousand?! Anyway I thought it was four thousand.

That's an interesting point in itself. There are actually two stories, one with five thousand and the other with four thousand. (Matt. 14:13-21 and 15: 32-39) Returning to your request, I find it more helpful to think in terms of people sharing what they had and finding they had more than enough to go round rather than God somehow multiplying the five loaves and two fish. In the other story they had seven loaves and a few small fish. Wouldn't it be wonderful if, today, people shared what they had instead of trying to accumulate more than enough? That would be a wonderful miracle if people didn't succumb to the temptation of greed.

Z: As my old grandad used to say, a man's riches is in direct proportion to the fewness of his wants. Your theory is all very well for a miracle but what about healing in the bible?

With regard to healing, nowadays, we tend to view things differently. Whereas in biblical times people who had a convulsive fit were thought to be possessed by demons the same symptoms are now diagnosed as an epileptic fit. If we have problems with our eyes the first line of action for all of us is to visit an optician.

Z: That's true. I rather have that than a local vicar rubbing spittle on!

All of us benefit from advances in science, particularly, advances in medical science. Indeed, it comes as something of a shock when people die at an early age because the presumption is that a cure can always be found and everybody will live to a great old age.

Z: Yes, you can get pills now for heart disease, blood pressure, slimming, and to improve your memory, not forgetting those that enhance your sex life!

I think we had better move on to another scientist. Charles Darwin undoubtedly rocked the ecclesiastical boat in the nineteen century when he published his tome, On the Origin of Species by Means of Natural Selection.

Z: This sounds like heavy stuff. I thought the origin of species was found in Genesis.

Yes, some people still think it is. Disturbingly, the movement know as Creationism seems to be gaining ground. This is the belief that the origins of the world and of mankind are more or less, as you say, found in the book of Genesis. On this view the world came into existence about six thousand years ago and is therefore totally incompatible with the Darwinian viewpoint. The latter asserts that human life has developed over millions of years. Scientists are trying to recreate the conditions one trillionth of a second after the origin of the universe at the Big Bang which is estimated to be 13.7 billion years ago! Some would argue that it is out of the question to believe in a God when creation began so long ago; that there is a God of the observable universe which has 100,000 million galaxies, each galaxy having 100,000 million stars. Others would argue that these vast figures and the very enormity of the universe are sufficient proof that there is a God. The universe works with such predictability that rockets can be sent to Mars which only arrive there many years later. Eclipses of the sun and moon can be predicted hundreds of years into the future with total accuracy. The tide ebbs and flows with such regularity that there are books of tide tables extending years into the future.

Other evidence for the age of the universe comes from the discoveries of geologists who cite the evidence of fossils. Creationists would argue that fossils and geological formations were all created by God at a particular date in time.

Z: I wonder why God would have wanted to do that?

Precisely! For me the problem with creationism is that it seems to deny the capacity of people to think. We have undoubtedly been given minds and, moreover, we are exhorted to believe with our hearts and souls <u>and minds</u>. It seems to me that creationism flies in the face of scientific facts among which are genetic discoveries that clearly link different species, and geological discoveries that clearly make the world millions of years older than the picture painted in Genesis. Maybe the fear is that if one part of the bible is seen to be not true, then maybe all of it is untrue.

Z: Once you start asking questions who knows where it will lead!

That's right, but the bible was not written as a scientific text book. Moreover, as we shall see later, there are other kinds of truth which are just as relevant as scientific truth. Another difficulty that Darwin inadvertently introduced is all to do with sin.

Z: Ah, I know quite a bit about that!

In classical theology it is maintained that sin entered the world through the actions of one man, namely, Adam. He was the one who succumbed to the words of the serpent..

Z: …..a talking serpent?....

and persuaded Eve to eat of the fruit of the tree of knowledge. Paul refers to Christ as the new Adam, 'for as all die in Adam, so all will be made alive in Christ'. (1 Cor. 15:22) This imagery is also found in Paul's letter to the Romans. "Therefore, just as sin came into the world through one man, and death through sin, and so death spread to all because all have sinned". (Roms. 5:12) In traditional terminology the sin of Adam is known as The Fall.

Z: Oh, I know all about falling!

No, this refers to THE Fall – the one act of Adam that resulted in the sin of human kind.

Z: So where does that leave Darwin and his theory of evolution?

Scientists the world over are now inclined to agree that Darwin was basically right with his theory of natural selection. The well known naturalist David Attenborough takes the theory as a given. This is the only explanation for the diverse species which his television programmes eloquently illustrate. The theory of Darwin suggests that the universe is still unfinished and therefore still incomplete. The point is that if we are continually evolving then we cannot have fallen from some state of perfection in the Garden of Eden. This being the case, we are not in some kind of fallen state from which we need to be rescued. We don't need to be rescued but rather, we are not the finished product. We are not yet fully human. The so-called theories of the atonement…..

Z: Just hold it there. Theories of the atonement? What is that all about?

Sorry Zeno. The word atonement is derived from the words, at-one-ment and is about reconciling two parties, that is, making them at one. In context it refers to the crucifixion of Jesus as a way of bridging the gap between God and 'fallen' men and women. The early Christians tried to make sense of the crucifixion of Jesus and so various theories were put forward.

Z: You mean theories about why Jesus died?

Exactly. For example, it was commonly thought at the time that sacrifices were necessary to put sin and the consequences of sin right. Consequently, Jesus was thought of as the perfect sacrifice whose death takes away the sin of the world. Another theory, called the penal substitution theory, says that humans have sinned and sin needs to be punished as a way of paying for the misdemeanour. There is no way that human beings can be reconciled to God without punishment for the sin being put into effect. The theory suggests that Jesus became a substitute for everybody and bore the punishment for all people and so reconciliation with God is possible. Another theory suggests that Adam failed to achieve his potential and lost the freedom which had been given to him. The only way this 'Fall' could be reversed would be for Jesus, the Second Adam, to resist temptation and evil and through his resurrection point the way to a new life which everybody could enter. In the light of evolution some of these theories need to be revisited if we are to make sense of the death of Jesus. For example, the paradigm of 'a second Adam to the fight and to the rescue came', no longer fits the bill. (1)

Z: I never did like that hymn, but at least it now makes a bit more sense. Anyway I'm not at all sure about any of these theories. It seems to me that Jesus was such a challenge to the religious authorities that he was bound to come to a sticky end.

At the turn of the last century, challenges to theology came from a different source, namely, the psychoanalyst Sigmund Freud.

Z: Now he was very interested in sex wasn't he?

Yes, he actually said that from a very early age we all have sexual inclinations, especially towards our parents. Apart from anything else, Freud developed the notion that we all have an unconscious part of ourselves. By definition, we are not aware of this but it makes itself known through such things as slips of the tongue, and through dreams. Freud reckoned dreams were the royal road to the unconscious.

The unconscious can also become more conscious through different kinds of psychoanalysis or counselling processes. The main point is that our egos are influenced by unconscious forces. Freud goes as far as to say that God is simply a projection of some of these forces. It is the human desire for comfort, the projection of an internal desire onto an external father figure, namely, God, in the midst of a hostile world. Consequently, God has no existence he is merely an illusion. Religion functions as a kind of neurosis. It has to be said, though, that a former colleague of Freud, Carl Gustav Jung, took a quite different approach and was in fact a firm believer in the existence of God. Jung often used religious symbols in his work and saw these as a powerful source of healing. However, the influence of Freud and his contention, derived from his psychoanalytic theory, that God is no more than an illusion, cannot be disputed.

Z: If God is an illusion then perhaps lots of things are? How do we know that anything exists? Anyway which of Freud's theories has any scientific credence? Wasn't he more of a poet than a scientist?

You aren't as daft as you seem Zeno because there is truth in what you say. However, the modern view is that science can solve everything. If there is a problem, then eventually there will be a scientific solution. If the world runs out of fossil fuel, not to worry, other kinds of energy will soon be found. If the world is in danger through climate change, not to worry, somebody will soon devise a way of reducing the detrimental effects of too many green house gases in the environment. If you are afflicted with Altzheimer's, not too worry, a cure is just around the corner. There is also the underlying assumption that science has actually, somehow, disposed of God.

Since God cannot be proved 'scientifically' then God can't possibly exist. The only things that exist are those which are accessible to our senses.

Z: You mean like custard pies?

I guess so but notice I used the word 'modern'. The optimism about scientific endeavour is a characteristic of the so called modern world, a world which began to take shape during the Renaissance, that is, the 14th to 16th centuries. Some of the other characteristics of this modern age are:-

- a belief in the power of reason and the power of individual minds. This implies a rejection of ecclesiastical authority and no longer submitting to it.
- a belief in progress; the belief that humans are capable of anything. All that is needed is courage, intelligence and effort and people can shape their own fate.
- As noted above there is a belief in science, especially the thought that nature can be

controlled and inventions made to subdue the forces of nature.

◆ There is no longer a preoccupation with the supernatural. The modern age is more concerned with the natural and that which can be observed.

◆ Above all else this is an age which is confident, buoyant and hopeful. This is an age which can solve problems and liberate people from ignorance, an age of justice and freedom.

Z: I have a funny feeling you are going to tell me that the modern age is no longer with us.

Indeed, some would argue that we are still living through this modern age. Others take the view that we are witnessing its death throes and we are now living in a post modern age. However, to define what is meant by post modern is like trying to hold dry sand, it just slips through your fingers.

Z: I have another funny feeling coming on. You are going to try and hold on to some sand. I'll try not to interrupt for a while so that you can concentrate on what you are doing.

The following are possible criteria for a post modern age.

1. Fragmentation. There is no longer a national bus company, or British Rail and the utilities are run by many different companies. Once upon a time there was one television channel which was transmitted by the BBC, now there is a plethora of channels. In a so-called Christian society there is now multi-faith teaching. Do people know what Pentecost is? What has happened to Good Friday? There are many different translations of the bible and many churches now

write their own liturgies and, literally, sing from their own hymn sheets. These examples are not given by way of value statements. They are simply a description of what is now happening in the West. Many other examples could be given of how, what could be argued were cohesive forces, have now become very fragmentary. Of course, it could be argued that other cohesive factors have sprung into life. The use of the English language is now very widespread and that is bound to aid communication. The world wide web and the use of the internet is also bringing people together in ways hitherto unheard of. Facebook and twitter are now common ways for people to interact. There are things like sacred space and other prayer web sites. People can even join a virtual church.

Z: That raises very interesting social and theological questions. Do they have a skeleton key in order to get in?

2. There is a certain disillusionment with science. Notwithstanding the many, many benefits of scientific discoveries, there has also been a negative impact. One example has been the effect of nuclear testing on the environment. So called progress has often been made to the detriment of ecological issues. Indeed, the wishes of local people have often been overlooked or over ridden in the name of progress. There is also the feeling that science has not solved many of the world's problems. Millions of people are still hungry, still lacking water and basic sanitation. In other words, where are the results of progress? Hunger and disease are still with us. Poverty abounds in large swathes of the world.

Z: Not to mention all the damage caused by oil pollution.

3. There is a search for something in life other than the natural or that which can be seen. Any book shop reveals large numbers of titles to do with 'new age' or 'spirituality'. Even if people are not going to church in the numbers they once did there is a great interest in 'the other'. When Princess Diana died, hundreds of people laid flowers outside her home, not only as a gesture of love and respect, but as a sign that they had been spiritually touched. One often sees wayside shrines that have been set up at the place of a road accident. Prime time television has had programmes such as 'The monastery' and 'Around the world in 80 faiths'. There is a feeling around, which many people find difficult to articulate, that there is more to this world than that which can be seen. The entirely rational world of modernity fails to satisfy the quest for the spiritual and mystical dimension in life. There is a desire for a different kind of truth as well as the scientific version.

4. Whereas the modern world was characterised by confidence the post modern world is characterised by doubt and uncertainty. There is a general mistrust and suspicion of institutions and various professions – lawyers, accountants, doctors, politicians, estate agents, even car mechanics. There is a mistrust especially of those who claim to have all the answers. There is no one answer that fits all but everything has become relative. 'It all depends'. Indeed, science itself has come to be mistrusted. For example, there are often conflicting views as to whether chocolate or red wine is good for ones health.

Z: Perhaps we need someone to say that most things are ok in moderation, especially chocolate.

When one considers the possible effects of global warming and climate change, not to mention the threat of terrorism, the future itself seems full of uncertainty. For some people, living with uncertainty is very difficult because of their psychological makeup. Clearly, something more that just the facts is needed.

Z: I'm always living with uncertainty. I just never know if people are going to laugh or not. I tell you it can feel a very vulnerable place to be.

It is a phenomenon which has been studied under experimental conditions and is called 'intolerance of ambiguity'. It is important for some to live in a world which is either black or white but not with shades of grey. Some Christians find certainty in an infallible pope or church leader, others in the pronouncements of their denomination, others in their own inner belief system whilst others place their faith in the bible, the supposedly unchangeable word of God.

The tendency is that the more a system of beliefs is unexamined the more rigid and defended it will be. However, we are challenged to believe not only with our hearts but with our minds as well. A little thought reveals that it is completely indefensible to adopt a literal interpretation of the bible. There are innumerable instances of how the bible, if taken literally, lands you in all sorts of trouble. Here are a few examples.

I would like to sell my daughter into slavery, as it suggests in Exodus 21:7.

Z: I hope you get a good price for her!

I have a neighbour who insists on working on the Sabbath. Ex.35:2 clearly states he should be put to death.

Z: Oh dear, I hope you don't feel obliged to kill him.

My son is drinking too much, when do I make arrangements to have him stoned? (Deut. 21:18-21)

Z: I think you are getting carried away.

If you can't control yourself you'd better get married. It is better to marry than burn with passion. (1 Cor 7:9)

Z: Back to sex again!! So marriage is a kind of legalizing of lust. Here's me thinking all sorts of lofty thoughts about marriage.

Could women also not dress with pearls or expensive clothes and could they please learn to keep silent. (1 Tim 2:9-12)

Z: I think I'm going to keep quiet. This feels like a can of worms!

In the 17th century Archbishop Ussher in Ireland published a chronology that purported the time and date of creation to be the night preceding 23rd October 4004 B.C. Radio carbon dating, fossil records and so on have shown that this date is out by a few million years! In similar fashion, it would be difficult to argue that Noah took two of every species on to his ark given that we now know there are millions and millions of different species.

Z: I wonder if there were any woodpeckers on the ark, or dinosaurs.

The bible is so easily misunderstood for what it is and is not. For all its inspiration, it is not primarily a history book and it is certainly not a scientific text book. The bible is not trying to answer the question how the world began for that is the realm of science.

Z: It's all very well to say what the bible isn't but what is it?

At one level the bible contains its own power and authority. The bible continues to have great impact on those who take the trouble to read it. The fact that people are touched, comforted, consoled, disturbed, inspired, uplifted by what they read is a testimony in itself. Historically, people like Martin Luther and John Wesley found it life changing to read Paul's letter to the Romans. Who has not been uplifted at a wedding service to hear the great hymn to love in 1 Corinthians 13 or been consoled at a funeral service with the words of psalm 23? My heart is always stirred when I hear the familiar words which begin the story of the birth of Jesus; 'in those days a decree went out from Emperor Augustus that all the world should be registered.' (Luke 2:1) This is a passage, incidentally, which gives a particular historical dating to the birth of Jesus. Further, as we shall see, Ignatius used biblical passages as a way of engaging the heart and not the head.

For me, problems arise when God is somehow locked into the pages on the bible. Certainly the bible contains the Word of God but God has continued to speak in various ways throughout the last two centuries. The bible is undoubtedly inspired and it has been written by inspired people but these people were human and, therefore, not infallible. They were also, inevitably affected by the culture in which they lived. It is not a requirement for Christians that they have to believe all they read in the bible from beginning to end. Discernment is vital. If there is no thinking, let alone discernment there is a danger that people will assume what the bible says.

For example, I heard recently of a mother who would not allow her child to eat apples because of 'what the bible says'. Presumably she was referring to the Garden of Eden incident where Adam was told by the serpent not to eat 'of the fruit of the tree that is in the middle of the garden'. (Gen 3:3).

Z: Perhaps her children also wore fig leaves in the appropriate places!

Notice that there is no reference to an apple. The story is about eating 'of the tree of the knowledge of good and evil'. (Gen. 2:17)

In a similar way every nativity play ever written mentions the inn keeper but there is no mention of him, or her, in the gospel account. Luke only mentions that there was no room in the inn. (Luke 2:7) Likewise the common assumption is that there were three wise men but the gospel only states that there were three gifts, gold, frankincense and myrrh. (Matt. 2:11) Three gifts could have been given by any number of people.

Z: That's so true. Sometimes I am fortunate to receive a number of birthday presents and they all come from just one person!

In any discussion of the bible it needs to be remembered that it is not one book in spite of appearances to the contrary! The bible is composed of sixty six books written at different times over a period of twelve hundred years, by different authors and written for different audiences. Moreover, there are different kinds of writing all of which need different ways of reading. For example, there are historical, prophetic and poetic books in the Old Testament. The way poetry is read and interpreted is quite different from the way in which a historical narrative is read. To say one is not true but the other is true misses the point entirely because there are different kinds of truth. There is historical truth, scientific truth, literal truth, and metaphorical truth and they are all needed if we are to make sense of our lives. When I tell a congregation that I can't speak properly because I have a frog in my throat, nobody believes that I have a real reptile in there somewhere!

Z: It would jump out with one leap!

Could it be said that the parable of the Good Samaritan is true? Was a man really attacked as he was on his way from Jerusalem to Jericho? This is not the important question for the story is a parable and as such contains another kind of truth. The parable was spoken by Jesus to answer the question 'who is my neighbour?' Similarly one does not have to think of Jonah in terms of a big fishy tale. Again, it is a parable and therefore by its very nature it contains truth but it does not have to be interpreted literally.

Z: But what about Adam and Eve? Were they historical figures or not?

I have to say that if people want to believe in a literal Adam and Eve and it makes them more holy and loving then who am I to argue.

Z: Who indeed!

This is not the important question because the story of the Garden of Eden is not about history any more than it is about a serpent that can talk or God who walks in the garden. The bible is more concerned with the question <u>why</u> the world began not <u>how</u> it began. Why is there anything here at all. Adam represents all people in that he finds it relatively easy to succumb to temptation and in doing so alienates himself from God. Indeed, this is one of the threads going throughout the Old Testament. People constantly rebel against God and fall away from trusting in him. Happily there is a way back because with God there is complete and total forgiveness. That is God's nature.

'If you, O Lord, should mark iniquities, Lord, who could stand?
But there is forgiveness with you'. (Psalm 130: 3,4, see also Isaiah 1:18)

Z: That's a relief then, especially for the likes of me.

Another thing to bear in mind when dealing with the bible is that authors in biblical times used a completely different technique than the one used nowadays. This book that I am writing is written by me using some references from elsewhere and hopefully, will be published at a particular point in time. The authorship of some biblical books is not precisely known except perhaps the books of the prophets in the Old Testament and most of the letters attributed to Paul in the New Testament. They were written over many years and were compiled from stories and sayings that had been preserved by people passing them on from mouth to mouth, the so called oral tradition. Indeed, they were often written years after the event. There are references above to the nativity story. Luke highlights the inn with no room and the shepherds abiding in the fields whereas Matthew highlights the story of the wise men and the massacre of the innocents. Luke was writing for a non Jewish audience and therefore wanted to emphasize the importance of the poor and the outsider, whereas Matthew was writing for a Jewish audience and therefore often cites Old Testament texts in his narrative.

Attitudes to the bible can often be polarized into either believing every word of it or, on the other hand, believing it is all rubbish. However, the text deserves time being given to it. For example, at one sitting, read through the gospel of Mark. It is just a few pages, a mere sixteen chapters.

Z: Are you seriously asking me to do that? You want me actually to read the bible?

Yes I do. You wouldn't expect to do your juggling by just reading a book about it. You learn it only through hours and hours of practice. So read the bible, in this case Mark's gospel. Allow the words to permeate. There is a very interesting point to note straight away. There is no mention of the birth of Jesus!

Z: No Christmas?

There are no shepherds, no wise men, no Mary and Joseph, nothing at all about what is traditionally called the nativity. I wonder why?

Z: Perhaps Mark hadn't heard of any of the birth stories. Perhaps he didn't think they were important.

Maybe Mark has a different focus, the death of Jesus, and he just wants to get on with his story. For whatever reason, Mark begins with the story of John the Baptist calling people to repent.

Z: Is the bible any use at all if there are so many questions about it?

Certainly one of the dangers is that we can read into it anything we want to. Thus, supporters of apartheid in South Africa were able to substantiate their position by the use of an obscure Old Testament text. Supporters of the just war theory and pacifists all use the bible to justify their claims. Jehovah's Witnesses are against the use of blood transfusions because of biblical injunctions. Clearly the bible is important because it is about how God has been perceived throughout the centuries. To that extent it is inspired and has much to teach us. More especially it is the major source of the records of the life of Jesus and the experiences of the early Christian church. However, as we have seen, each book of the bible has to be taken on its own merits. What kind of writing is it? What context was it written in? Who was it written for? and so on. The bible is not the be all and end all of faith. We have to use our reason and our experience and have some knowledge of what the tradition of the church has to say. Ultimately the key question is, what do these words of the bible that I am reading have to say to me now.

Z: Maybe we could even disagree with tradition.

I would certainly hope so, and also use our experience and knowledge so that we do not rely solely on the bible. It has nothing to say, specifically, for example, about life in a welfare state, about artificial insemination, organ transplants, nuclear power or space travel. All these things would have been beyond the imagination of biblical writers. Conversely, some things in the bible are now regarded as relevant to that culture but not to ours. For example the wearing of hats by women in church (1 Cor. 11:10) is now rarely observed. I guess many Christians eat bacon and pork without thinking about it but it was certainly forbidden to the Jews. (Lev. 11: 7-8) Times continue to change and, thankfully, God continues to be revealed to us. God cannot be encased in the pages of the bible.

Z: That would be very funny, trying to limit almighty God to a particular time capsule.

Yes, God is far too important to be consigned to the pages of history. The bible is not written by God and then dropped down from heaven. More is it a collection of people's responses to what they perceived as the activity of God in their lives and in the society around them. People cannot live as Christians as though major scientific discoveries have not been made otherwise there is a danger of becoming spiritually schizophrenic. There is the very real danger of believing one thing on Sunday but as soon as Monday morning comes round living in a different kind of world. It becomes a sort of Jekyll and Hyde existence; Jekyll on Sunday and Hyde every other day of the week.

God cannot truly and honestly be worshipped if it is thought that the earth is still the centre of the universe or that people live in a three decker universe with heaven up above, hell down below and us in the middle. God cannot be worshipped as though there have not been any scientific insights over the last few hundred years. Indeed, even in a generation the changes have been breathtaking. I grew up after World War II in a home with no television, no central heating, no fridge, no washing machine, no car, no computer and certainly no mobile phone.

Z: How did you survive?

Sometimes I wonder. Not only is the bible a means of comfort, a provider of spiritual strength, and the place where we can read of the life of Jesus and the wonderful, stirring story of the early Christians, it is also life changing. (2) If we read it with care and attention we soon discover the ways in which God has communicated with people over many years, especially in the life of Jesus. The question for us now, is how does God communicate with people in this day and age?

## **Points to Ponder:**

1. Does the theory of evolution undermine the traditional view of the Christian faith?

2. What do you make of Freud's idea that God is merely a projection?

3. Do you think that God ever suspends the laws of nature? Why?

4. In what ways is the bible important for you? Which passages speak directly to you?

5. When have been the occasions when you have perceived God acting in your life?

# Meditation:

An Ignatian contemplation takes the form of prayer recommended by Ignatius of Loyola. It consists in taking a scene from the life of Christ and reliving it. That is, by imagining that you are actually in the scene as if it were actually occurring and you are a participant in the event. The process is best explained by way of example.

Read a passage of scripture e.g. the story of Martha and Mary in Luke 10: 38-42

Now spend some time quietening yourself as preparation. Do an awareness exercise e.g. be aware of your breathing and know that God is closer to you than your breathing.

Now imagine yourself into the village. What is it like? What is the weather like? How are you feeling? Have you travelled far? Now imagine that you are in the home of Martha and Mary. Can you describe the home? What is it like?..... is there a fire?.....any furniture? ....are there any animals around?.....how big is it?.....is it tidy?.......clean?......are there any smells?.......how many rooms are there?.......is there an upstairs?.............

Now imagine that into this house comes Jesus with some of his disciples...........what is the atmosphere?....where have they come from?.....are they tired?.....hungry?....... thirsty?.........is there much conversation?.........

Try not to observe the scene from outside as an observer but imagine that you are actually present in the home of Martha and Mary. What are you doing there? What are your feelings? Are you in the same room as Jesus or in the

kitchen? Do you speak to anyone? To whom?..........Do they reply?........What are you feeling?
Spend some time in this scene..........finally spend a few more moments in the presence of Jesus in quiet prayer.......

Slowly return to the room in which you began the exercise, in your own time open your eyes. Be aware of the people and the noises around you, be aware of yourself – say your own name to yourself.

Note that this kind of contemplation is not easy and is not for everybody. It may be a case of 'if at first you don't success then try again'. You will probably fare better at a second attempt.

Some people tend to object that this is not a theological way or an historical way of approaching the gospel narratives. This method however is a way of entering the text in a mystical way. It is one way of making the text come alive and for many people it works. By being present in the scene and often by identifying with one of the participants, Martha, Mary, a disciple, a bystander, they become aware of their own feelings and what it means to be present with Jesus.

Of course the meditation must be entered into in an attitude of faith, in the belief that God only desires that which is good for us and that God is ready to speak through our hearts. Then you are in a position to attain the truth of mystery. If you become part of the story God will speak into your heart, your reality.

# References

1. Hymns and Psalms, 231

2. Since the end of the Cultural Revolution in 1976, when the bible was banned, confiscated and burned, it has become China's bestseller. It is even printed in China rather than smuggled into the country. In 2009, four million bibles were printed and distributed in China. One woman said 'reading the bible is like having God talk to you.' <u>Word in Action</u>, Bible Society, Summer, 2010

Further Reading:
Barton, John, <u>What is the Bible?</u> SPCK, 1991
Rodd, C.S., <u>The Bible</u>, Epworth, 1996

# Chapter 3

## Problems with prayer

An obvious way in which people communicate with God is through prayer the trouble is that I, for one, do not find praying particularly easy. I can offer a series of words but prayer is surely far more than uttering some words. I was greatly encouraged when I found the following quotation in a book called 'How to Pray'.

'After sixty-three years of life and thirty-eight years of priesthood, my prayer seems as dead as a rock.......I have lived with the expectation that prayer would become easier as I grow older and closer to death. But the opposite seems to be happening. The words 'darkness' and 'dryness' seem best to describe my prayer today.... Are the darkness and dryness of my prayer signs of God's absence, or are they signs of a presence deeper and wider than my senses can contain? Is the death of my prayer the end of my intimacy with God or the beginning of a new communion, beyond words, emotions, and bodily sensations?' (1)

Note that these words were written by Henri Nouwen, a

well-known spiritual writer who has inspired thousands of people.

Z: I guess there is hope for you then in your pathetic efforts at prayer.

Hope springs eternal as they say! One of the major problems with prayer is that for many people there never seems to be any time! It's not that people reject God it's more that they can't find enough time, or indeed, any time for God.

Z: You mean prayer has become an optional extra rather than a basic necessity?

That's right. The problem is that this results in feelings of guilt and my guess is that God is not found through feelings of guilt but by a real desire to find God. Spiritual growth comes not from any feelings of obligation but from passion and desperation. So often, religious language is couched in the language of 'ought' and 'should'. These are punishing words and not helpful aids on our spiritual journey. There are no dos and don'ts when it comes to the life of prayer. In the words of the well known aphorism, you pray as you can not as you can't.

Z: What if I don't feel like praying at all?

Many moons ago C.S. Lewis wrote, ' Faith......is the art of holding on to things your reason once accepted, in spite of your changing moods. For moods will change, whatever view your reason takes.'(2) Indeed, sometimes things happen in a positive way if we do things when we are not in the mood. If we only did things when we were in the right mood or when we just felt right I don't think we would achieve very much at all. The main thing in prayer is that we don't try to be what we are not.

Many years ago, when I was a teacher the school was to be visited by the Queen.

Z: Was that Victoria?

Very funny Zeno. I was struck by all the preparation that went into her visit. Graffiti was scrubbed away, flowers and bushes planted, litter removed, rooms painted, and pupils and teachers were on their best behaviour. The Queen, being an official visitor, never sees things as they are. The point is that God is not an official visitor. God sees us precisely as we are so there is no point in trying to be something other than we are. Therefore we pray as we are, not as we aren't. Furthermore, prayer is not an examination. You don't need a theology degree to speak to God anymore than you need a medical degree to speak to a doctor. Prayer is for amateurs and we remain amateurs all our lives.

Z: I like that idea.

Then there are those who pray to God in a torrent of words. There will be more later on the topic of silent prayer but for the moment it is as well to remember some words of Jesus; ' when you are praying, do not heap up empty phrases as the Gentiles do; for they think that they will be heard because of their many words. Do not be like them, for your Father knows what you need before you ask him.' (Matt. 6: 7-8) Jesus then goes on to give the wonderfully succinct Lord's Prayer as a model for all to copy.

Z: Did you know that in St. Michael-le-Belfrey church in York the Lord's Prayer is written in full on one of the screens at the back of the altar? However, the writer had difficulty getting each phrase onto a separate line so he wrote 'Our Father which art in heaven, hallo'.

Actually, Zeno, although you don't realise it, you have made a very good point. How comfortable are we in the presence of God? Certainly in the Old Testament people were afraid of God. For example, Moses had to approach God at the top of a mountain. In the temple in Jerusalem, a specially chosen priest was the only one who could approach God in the Holy of Holies. A different face of God is shown when we look upon the birth of a baby in Bethlehem.

Z: God must be very courageous to take the form of a baby and become so vulnerable and dependent. I also like to think that God has a sense of humour. After all he asked you to be one of his ministers!

I can't argue with that but let's return to praying! Our prayers are often in the form of requests. The requests may well not be for our self, but they are nevertheless requests. Please can you help my neighbour who is in hospital? Can you do something about the plight of people in the Sudan? How long does the war in Afghanistan have to go on for until you do something about it? Our church roof is leaking can you please help us to raise all the money we need to repair it? Our minister is leaving, can you please make sure we have a good replacement?

Z: At the end of his sermon the minister told his congregation that Jesus had called him to another parish. The congregation then lustily sang 'What a friend we have in Jesus'.

It is so easy to treat God as though he were a Father

Christmas kind of figure who simply hands out goodies to all and sundry. How many times are our prayers about asking for something? The danger is that prayer simply becomes an ego trip, all about my preoccupations and what I want. We all fall under the illusion from time to time that we are the centre of the universe and everything revolves round us.

All the requests underlie a tendency to perceive God as the great magician of the skies.

Z: There's an image to conjure with. What's the magic word?

All God needs to do, we think, is wave a magic wand and all will be well. That might be all very well in theory but the practice is quite different. In any case, if God intervened at our every whim what would happen to our sense of moral responsibility? God is not going to do something if we are not prepared to do something for ourselves. The war in Afghanistan, for example, will not end unless there is a desire among politicians for it to end. Furthermore if we ask God to intervene and stop it why in heaven's name does God not intervene earlier and thus prevent thousands of deaths? The bible does not say that God will intervene to change this and that but there is a promise that God will be with us through thick and thin. Centuries ago a similar sentiment was uttered by Julian of Norwich

> He did not say
>> 'You shall not be tempest – tossed,
>> You shall not be work-weary,
>> You shall not be discomforted'.
> But he said
>> 'You shall not be overcome'. (3)

Underlying the above kinds of 'asking' prayer lies the presumption that we, as mere mortals, can act as spiritual advisors to the Almighty.

Z: That is quite a claim but I guess it is much easier to act as an advisor to someone rather than actually get your own hands dirty. I could advise someone what to do with their money, for example, give it to me, then I wouldn't have to work for a living!

We know what is best for our neighbour, or so we think, and we do not hesitate to tell God what needs to be done. We know what is required to put the church to rights and the world on a more secure footing and so we tell God what action to take.

Our prayers are often telling God what to do about a particular world situation or about Mrs. Smith next door who is really quite ill and would benefit from the Almighty's attention. The question is does she want to recover or does she feel as though her life on this earth has come to an end and she is ready to meet her Maker? Prayer can also be very oppressive. If Mrs Smith is in a hospice waiting and wanting to die it can become very difficult for her if she knows that people are praying for her recovery. Jesus, when confronted with a blind man, does not rush in to cure him. He asks him, 'what do you want me to do for you?' (Mark 10:51) At first blush it seems obvious what the man wanted but Jesus makes no assumptions.

On another occasion Jesus meets an ill man by a pool in Jerusalem. Again, Jesus asks the question, 'do you want to be made well?' (John 5:6) The man had been ill for thirty eight years and therefore he had a particular life style which revolved around his disability. He had become dependent on others for his survival. What would happen if he suddenly regained full health and strength?

Z: No wonder Jesus asked him; the thought of new life must have seemed very risky.

Many kinds of prayers I have no difficulty with. I can say thank you, say I am sorry, ask for forgiveness and praise God quite readily.

Z: That's a bit of progress then.

The prayer I have most difficulty with is intercession. What precisely is happening when I am praying for other people or situations? There are all sorts of difficulties.

I remember many years ago, when the Vietnam conflict was at its height, going to a service at which Sydney Carter was speaking.

Z: Is that the same guy who wrote 'Lord of the Dance' and 'When I needed a neighbour'?

The very same. Before saying anything, he displayed a map of the world and then asked the congregation to point to Vietnam. That proved to be impossible for many people. Over the years we had engaged many times with preachers as they prayed for Vietnam but we couldn't even locate the country on a map. Were we in danger of simply handing over a problem to God in the hope that God would solve it? Maybe we are in danger of doing the same today with our countless prayers during the last decade about the Middle East, Iraq and Afghanistan. All too easily we can evade our responsibility and pray for a situation without knowing anything at all about the issues involved.

Did you know, Zeno, that the UK has the highest per capita spending on the military in Europe and is second in the world only to the United States. The UK exports £5 billion of military equipments around the globe, often to countries which could be described as underdeveloped.

Z: No doubt those same countries are being supported by aid agencies like Christian Aid or Tearfund.

Absolutely. Ironic isn't it? For example, India is ranked 128th out of 177 countries on the Human Development Index with an estimated 40% of the country living in abject poverty. Nevertheless, the UK exported £90m of military equipment to India in 2006 and £130m in 2007.

Z: In other words praying for peace or the eradication of poverty in the third world might entail a bit more than pious words to God.

Precisely. The latest piece of military equipment is called the drone. These are unmanned aircraft that fire missiles by remote control that are run by operators sitting in front of computer screens thousands of miles away from the front line.

Z: Perhaps one day, if people continue to wage war, they will be waged on computer screens like a computer game.

Perhaps so but in the meantime, the arms industry seems to feed economic inequalities and it is precisely these inequalities that can lead to more conflicts. On another subject, I am constantly struck by the amount of news footage given over to climate change. The polar ice cap is melting at a rapid rate. The Innuit people are facing major changes in their lives and polar bears seem to be facing extinction. The Maldive islands are threatened with imminent flooding as are other low lying areas. Yet, in spite of all these regular warnings I often come across people who repeatedly fly for pleasure. I heard of a school that is arranging for its pupils to go on a rugby tour to New Zealand and a hockey tour to South Africa. Is it really necessary to fly to such distant places purely for sport? Many people seem unable to make the connection between climate change and their own particular life style. It goes without saying that we only have one world and if we don't look after it nobody else will, not even God.

Z: Whoa there boy. You are getting on your high horse and that's not a comfortable place to be. Just because you recycle as much as possible, collect your rain water and have solar panels doesn't make you perfect. I know for a fact that you drive far too fast. You could save petrol and the environment by driving a bit slower.

Thanks for that Zeno! That apart, is God going to intervene and change situations that people could change for themselves?

Z: When you go jogging and you have to cross a road it's no good praying there will be lots of traffic so you can have a rest. If you need a rest, just stop running.

Yes. There are many things we can do for ourselves so there is no point in praying about it. This raises the major question of how God acts to answer our prayers. For example, does God have the power to step in and stop wars? Many prayers were offered to prevent the invasion of Iraq, not to mention major demonstrations on the streets of London and other cities but, apparently, God did not intervene to prevent the war.

Z: If I remember rightly, you went on that antiwar demonstration in London.

Yes I did. People could say that God has answered prayers and intervened because the invading forces have withdrawn and there is peace but I would want to ask why didn't God do something sooner and intervene in the thought processes of Mr. Bush and Mr. Blair. At what point precisely does God deem it fit to intervene? It seems to me that God intervenes through people, through their thoughts and feelings. This was certainly my experience on a silent retreat. The necessary prerequisite though, is that we have to be open and receptive to that possibility. Mr. Blair was interviewed on his return from a conversation with Mr Bush and asked if they had prayed together. This would be a reasonable thing for two Christians to do. Apparently they did not pray together.

Z: Perhaps history would have taken a different course if they had taken time out to listen to God and their inner voices. What seems crazy to me is that people still think in a supposedly civilised world that a good way to solve a dispute is by killing lots of innocent people. I thought the bible that you keep telling me about says quite categorically, 'You shall not murder'. Even if you call it by a fancy name like collateral damage, war seems to me like legalised murder.

Thanks for that Zeno. You have really gone to town there. It's unlike you to get so stirred up and use so many words. Of course, you make a good point but some would argue that you are over simplifying although I have to say that I actually agree with you. A paramount instruction in the New Testament is to love our neighbour. It is difficult to love someone if you are trying to kill them. If only we could see that we are all part of the same human family.

Z: Could you have a go at answering the question whether God answers prayer?

Traditionally the reply is that God does answer all our prayers. The reply can be 'no', 'yes', or 'not yet'.

Z: Could I include a fourth possible answer? 'You must be joking.'

I think there may be some truth in that reply! Although we read in the New Testament that God is concerned with the hairs of our head, moreover God is concerned about us because God is a God of love, there are some things we pray for which are blatantly selfish and serve our own ends. We pray for fine weather so that we can have a good day out by the seaside but the farmer down the road is desperately praying for rain for his crops. We pray for 'journeying mercies' but that is of little avail if we haven't bothered to check our car tyre pressures or ensure that the car has enough petrol, oil and water. It is in cases like this, I think, that God says 'you must be joking'. God is not a conjuror who waves a magic wand and suddenly changes the weather or apparently decides, at random, that the people in the car crash are not going to be injured. It would be a very unpredictable world if I fell and didn't bruise myself just because I had said my prayers that morning. 'Lest we sink into magic thinking, however, where God becomes a big jukebox prayer wheel and our prayers the coins that operate the machine, we must remember that sometimes the events that answer or parallel our praying are not ones we will greet with enthusiasm. Prayers are sometimes answered by the experience of more struggle, by our being plunged into situations where we must risk more than we ever dared before.' (4) Rather than wave a magic wand I think God promises something much more important. God promises to be with us in whatever situation we find ourselves. That seems to me to be much more helpful and, indeed, more faithful to the New Testament record. The future can be lived through because God is there with us and the past cannot be changed, although it can be forgiven.

One way of looking at prayer is making our self present to God and the transforming effect that presence has. Prayer then becomes the response to God's action in my life and God's presence within me

Ulanov argues that we may have missed something important if we are content with an obvious answer to our prayer. Particularly is this the case when we come to the complex issues involved in suffering. There may well be a prayer of gratefulness when there is a temporary cessation of pain, or, indeed, a permanent return to a sense of wholeness but what is remarkable when the suffering does not cease is that 'we find ourselves more able to endure the lack of wholeness which characterises the human condition. Our prayers are answered, then, by an enlargement of our capacity to suffer and to accept suffering as an indelible part of our lives and of the lives of others. We are thrust more into the world and we are more vulnerable to its pain.' (5)

Neville Ward writes that 'the answer to prayer that matters most is the general result which prayer is expected and intended to achieve, the purpose for which prayer is used; and this is the expression and deepening of our faith in

God, our desire for the coming of his rule in our perplexing world and our love for him and his created world of infinitely interesting persons and things. If prayer does not do this for us, after a reasonable trial, it is a waste of time and should be abandoned for more fruitful activities. Life is just too short to waste time praying if praying does not lead one to love life and enjoy it more.' (6)

Z: The idea of loving life and enjoying it more seems a great idea.

Ward goes so far as to suggest 'there is no such thing as unanswered Christian prayer. But because God works his will through persons, the answers wait on the availability of persons willing to carry them out. There are always *some* people ready to be vehicles of God's purpose, but sometimes we all sink into despair because, as Jesus put it, the labourers are so few for the harvest of God's inscrutable love, and among these few we so rarely see ourselves.' (7) As we have seen, this is how God intervenes, through people. Ward believes therefore that God answers all our prayers *even* when praying for things like the peace of the world.

Another important answer or function of prayer is that it protects us from ourselves. In a culture which prides itself on what humans have achieved and what they can do for themselves prayer acts as a corrective to our desire to do everything. 'Prayer protects us from our pretensions to omnipotence, our inflated conviction that we can do it all, by connecting us to a larger source which really can do everything.' (8) This is a good corrective in preventing exhaustion and burn out. Even if we stop, the world continues to go round and God continues to work in millions of different ways.

Z: I think you have left something out. There is another

way in which God answers prayers. I think God says 'do you really mean it?'

Yes, that's right. A good example would be praying for lots of young people to come into church. Do you really mean it? Will you like it if they are noisy? Will you appreciate any new ideas they bring? Will you be able to join in their songs or will you reject them out of hand? Are you really, really sure you want young people in your congregation?

Z: Older people often want younger people in church but only when they are grown up?! Talking of children, they are taught by adults to share, to be honest and not to bully. I wonder why it is that adults don't follow their own advice.

I'm afraid I can't answer that. Returning to the original point, another example would be to pray for the advancement of the ecumenical movement so that churches come closer together. Do you really, really mean it? What would you say if it meant the closure of your church? What would you say if it meant there was one church and one denomination in your town? Are you prepared to accept the changes that would naturally occur if churches began working together? What would you say if 'Churches Together' in your town or area, decided on the kind of minister for your church or that your church should be the one to close?

Z: That is getting very close to the bone! I remember the story of sailors that discovered someone living on a desert island. The captain noticed that the lone person had built a variety of buildings including two churches. On being asked why he had built two churches, the reply was 'the other one is the one I don't go to'.

The moral is that it is all very well to pray for this that and the other but have we really worked through the implications of our prayers being answered? My fear is that this kind of prayer seemingly lets us off the hook. We have prayed for what is perceived to be the Christian thing but the reality is that we have passed our responsibility on to God. No wonder our prayers are not answered in the way we would like. Prayers don't work unless we do!

Z: Can you give me some examples.

Quite simply it's no good expecting God to help old Mrs. Smith across the road if we are not prepared to help in some way. Perhaps we could visit her and have a cup of tea, do some shopping for her, ring her up or whatever.

Z: Are you saying that God doesn't do anything at all?

I am simply saying that very often the answer to our prayers often lies within our self. There is the potential for God to act where ever there are people.

Z: Does God appear on Facebook then?

I think he is on it all the time if people are actively engaging with each other at a deep level, sharing their lives and having some fun. If you can forgive the attempt at a joke, a different answer might be that God has given us his Face in Jesus. Every culture tends to find a different face for God:- a Victorian Father, a Man for Others, a film star like Robert Powell in the film, Jesus of Nazareth, a clown as in the musical Godspell.

Z. Now you are talking my kind of language!
What we have to do is to discover who Jesus is for us as

individuals and check that out from what we know of him from other sources – the bible, the church, our reason and our experience.

Z: What about twitter then?

Well I'm in two minds about that.

Z: Sounds like you are schizophrenic.

I am genuinely in two minds. Does God really hear our twitterings? The bible does say that even the hairs of our head are numbered and that gives the impression that God is intimately concerned with our daily lives. On the other hand I can't help feeling that God is only concerned with the bigger issues in life.

Z: But what constitutes a bigger issue? It reminds me of a certain newspaper!

Well that is a good example. When there are so many homeless people in the world, refugees with nowhere to call home, do I really want God to be concerned about my silly twitterings? It seems selfish in the extreme for me to be praying for a fine day so that I can have a barbecue with my family when people in Ethiopia haven't seen any rain at all for two years!! If God were in control of the weather I would fervently entreat him to pour some water into large swathes of the African continent.

All this still leaves the basic question of what happens when we are interceding for someone. Is it legitimate to pray for Uncle Fred's bunion? What are we praying for when we know that someone has cancer or that a marriage is in danger of breaking up? Are we telling God something that is already known? Are we expecting to persuade God to have a change of mind and thereby change the course of history? Are we prompting God to engage in an act of love and compassion when, generally, God is thought of as being all loving? To put it quite simply, does God respond to our intercession by acting in a particular way or does God act by getting us to change our minds?

Some would argue forcibly that God does respond even when there is evidence to the contrary. God has acted but not in the way we thought. A miracle has not happened but 'I know God has responded'. This seems to me a little unsatisfactory because it's a case of God always wins. This is the case of faith, of hoping against hope.

Z: Perhaps God always wins because God is God!

Well it's not as easy as that. Consider people in concentration camps during World War II – or indeed the lives of the early Christian martyrs. Many prayers must have been said on their behalf yet God seemed powerless to intervene.

Of course, some will argue that they have witnessed the intervention of God in their own lives and in the lives of others. I was once taking a shower and I distinctly heard a voice saying 'go and visit your mother'. This was a complete surprise. The voice came out of nowhere. I knew my mother was not too well. As far as I knew, all she had was a heavy cold and so I had no plans to visit since she lived two hundred miles away. Nevertheless, I dropped everything and went to see her. The following day she was admitted to hospital and two days later she died.

Z: Perhaps you should take a shower more often if you want to hear God.

Then there are those people who have 'seen' a miraculous healing. Who is to argue with them? Tennyson agrees with this sentiment when he writes in his poem Morte D'Arthur ' more things are wrought by prayer than this world dreams of'.

The problem is that if we take the view that God heals some people and not others then that seems to be a very arbitrary way of acting. Will God act in that way even if we don't bother to pray at all? One could freely cite examples of non-Christians who have been saved from apparent disaster and yet no prayers were uttered for their survival. Does God act in an arbitrary fashion?

Anthony de Mello says that, in reality, we never know what is good or what is bad for our neighbour. To support this view he tells a story about 'good luck' and 'bad luck'. It is actually very difficult to say what is bad luck or good luck. Who knows? Of course, certain kinds of behaviour are bad and unacceptable but 'to be honest, we just don't know what is good and what is bad for anybody and that, in the midst of our humble limitations, should give us great peace at the time of taking decisions. We are not burdened with the responsibility to solve all problems for everybody and to ensure the universal welfare of mankind.... God is the one who will change the bad luck into good in his providence'. (9)

Z: This is all very well but I thought that Paul says in your bible that you should always make your requests known to God.- who knows our needs before we put them into words! Aren't Christians encouraged to 'take it to the Lord in prayer?'

Very good Zeno. The very act of praying can alter the way we think and feel. You are actually thinking of the verse 'Do not worry about anything, but in everything by prayer and supplication with thanksgiving let your requests be made known to God'. (Phil. 4:6) I'm certainly not one to argue with St. Paul but when he says 'requests' I don't think he had a Christmas present list in mind. For a start he never mentions Christmas.

Z: Even I know that. Christmas wasn't celebrated till about three hundred years after the birth of Jesus.

I think that Paul has in mind the things of the spirit; those special things that really energise us spiritually. The ultimate gift for Paul is to be 'in Christ'. Nothing else matters. I think that Jesus has these spiritual qualities in mind when he says, ' Ask, and it will be given to you; search, and you will find; knock, and the door will be opened for you'. (Matt. 7:7)

Jesus implies that we can have the same relationship with his Father as he does. The important thing, though, is the nature and the depth of this relationship. Very little is said about the content of the prayers of Jesus. There are no instances of Jesus, for example, praying for the Roman Empire or that the Roman occupation may soon be over. We read that he often went away to a quiet place to pray but there is no record of the content of these prayers except in the last discourse of the fourth gospel where Jesus prays that his disciples may 'all be one'. A few hours before he was crucified, Jesus also prayed in the Garden of Gethsemane in extreme adversity as he was sweating drops of blood 'nevertheless let thy will be done'. Indeed these are the words at the heart of the Lord's Prayer.

Z: Does God have a will? If that is the case where does that leave human freedom?

Quite so. The implication is that God's will is fixed and final rather like the lines in a play and all that believers have to do is to learn the lines and all will be well. Sometimes people talk about the will of God as if it were a never-changing blue-print of what God 'wants' to happen in the world. This can produce difficulties for the believer who tries to discover the lines and learn them and then suffers pangs of guilt or remorse if it is thought that the lines are not the correct ones. Furthermore, this scenario implies that God's will is intransigent. That God only has one will. If that is the case, where indeed, does that leave human freedom? In one sense prayer presumes that we have choices and, more than that, we have the freedom to choose.

Z: Is there such a thing as freedom?

Good question Zeno. We are coming to that in a later chapter.

Z: Let me ask another question then. Is there any concret evidence to suggest that God answers prayer?

On the face of it one might expect that science would come up with some evidence. Technically, if prayer affects things in the physical world, its effects should be measurable, and science should be able to investigate it.

Baelz quotes an early scientific study of Galton on the effectiveness of prayer. Sovereigns have been prayed for every week in the Church of England since the book of common prayer came into existence in 1662. From statistics available for the years 1758 to 1843 Galton discovered that 'sovereigns are literally the shortest lived of all who have the advantage of affluence' and he concluded that the prayer, "Grant her in health long to live", had no efficacy 'unless the very questionable hypotheses be raised, that the conditions of royal life may naturally be yet more fatal, and that their influence is partly, though incompletely, neutralized by the effect of public prayers'. (10) Certainly, in spite of all the hundreds of thousands of prayers, the present royal family has been through a number of difficult times. It seems to me that there are many more examples as well as the royal family where prayers have been said but the situation has continued. The last two World Wars would meet my point. Not to mention that people on both sides were praying for victory. The German soldier carried on his belt the motto –*Gott mit uns* – God with us.

Z: Which side was God on? Does God take sides?

I don't think God can ever be on the side of war but that is another issue altogether. Let's return to the original question. Dossey, in a recent book, has brought together a large number of interesting experiments with challenging results.(11) Out of 131 controlled experiments on prayer-based healing, more than half showed statistically significant benefits. One of the best known is a double blind study of 393 patients in the coronary unit at San Francisco General Hospital. In this experiment, 192 patients, chosen at random, were prayed for by home prayer groups, the others were not. The prayed-for patients recovered better than the controls, and fewer died. It is difficult for science to make sense of this data because it has a strictly mechanistic view of the universe based on cause and effect.

To begin to argue about the effectiveness of prayer is to enter the sphere of empirical science. This is not the life of faith. As Baelz argues, 'God is not a mechanism to be set in action by a verbal shilling in the slot......if the question, " what is the use of prayer?", means only, "Does it produce the goods?", the questioner has abandoned the sphere of religion for that of the market place'. (12)

For Baelz, prayer is not open to scientific study because that is not what prayer is about. Prayer essentially 'stems from the expression and cultivation of this attitude of dependence. It is the conscious surrender of ourselves to God, come what may'. (13) To state the obvious, prayer is about our relationship to God that goes beyond the limitations of normal human relationships. It is in prayer that we are apprehended by God. Not that we can control this. Any encounter with God is up to God, not us. All we can do is be open and aware of the possibility that God may encounter us at any moment. This 'encounter is beyond our comprehension. It does not take place through our conscious rational minds. It is an encounter of the feeling heart, not of the thinking mind'. (14)

Within this encounter the very least we want to do is mention other people and situations. The late Archbishop Michael Ramsay described intercession as 'being with God with others on our heart'. (15) As Pritchard writes 'the best and biggest thing we can do for anyone, is to hold them before God and expose them to the power of love, the power which, after all makes and sustains the world. So saying that we'll pray for someone is a serious commitment to loving that person enough to take them regularly to God.' (16)

Some of the difficulties of intercessory prayer disappear if we can think of it in a slightly different way. 'It is helpful to see intercession not so much as making requests of God, or asking him to do things, but as a way of co-operating with him. If we recognize that God is active in his world to further his purpose, prayer is a way of sharing in this activity.' (17) Ward writes, 'every Christian prayer for others involves the realization that he who prays is inextricably bound up with the answer. His prayer is not a mere message sent to God, voicing a request. It carries him with it deep into all that costly action which is the purpose of God in the life of the world. If it is not this it is simply the crying of a child.' (18)

Pritchard says something similar. Praying for the world and people in it 'is no less than joining in God's majestic project to transform the world....it's making ourselves part of God's massive attack on evil and on everything that destroys, distorts or cramps human life.' (19) In our prayers of intercession we are joining in a campaign of love that, of course, will ultimately change us. The answer to our prayers may well lie within ourselves as we become agents of God's loving purposes. 'God does not need to be told anything about what we need or want. Our words in prayer are not for God's instruction but our own. We discover this way what in fact we do desire, what we want to reach out to and love.' (20)

Not that any of this is easy. Prayer is a struggle. It is all too easy to give up when the going gets touch, utter a few platitudes and rush off to the next activity. It is as though prayer is just another activity amongst many. Along with the daily round, a cup of coffee, a quick chat we throw in a few seconds for a prayer. This leaves no time to get in touch with God let alone develop a meaningful relationship and can ultimately be deeply dissatisfying leaving us with an emptiness and an unfulfilled desire.

In conclusion, prayers of intercession are hard work. Within the context of a church service, it is all too easy to trip the words off the tongue but to what effect? Can we be more open to what God is asking of us? Can we find time to be quiet? Can we do the hard work of being better informed? More particularly, as we lift before God our loving concerns, can we resist the temptation of telling God what course of action to take. Ultimately, however, I want to admit with Paul, that although I do not know how to pray, I continue with the confident assurance that 'the Spirit helps us in our weakness; for we do not know how to pray as we ought, but that very Spirit intercedes with sighs too deep for words....and we know that all things work together for good for those who love God, who are called according to his purpose.' (Roms 8: 26, 28 NRSV)

Z: You have mentioned once or twice the idea of being quiet. If I shut up, is that prayer?

Sometimes I wish you would but that brings us to the idea of silence in prayer.

## Points to Ponder:

1. What experiences have you had of God answering prayer?

2. Prayers of intercession are sometimes like a Cook's tour of the world. What other ways of praying for other people might be more effective?

3. Prayer has been described as making ourselves present to God and then being transformed by that presence. How does this help you in your prayer life?

4. Another description is prayer as the response to God's action in my life and his presence within me. How do you respond to that?

5. List some positive things about prayer or is prayer 'just a complete waste of time'?

## Meditation:

Read very slowly twice the following; 'come to me, all you that are weary and are carrying heavy burdens, and I will give your rest. Take my yoke upon you, and learn from me; for I am gentle and humble in heart, and you will find rest for your souls. For my yolk is easy, and my burden is light'. (Matt. 11: 28) Mull over one word, or a phrase that speaks to you. What might God be saying to you in that word or phrase?

# References

1. Pritchard, John, <u>How to Pray</u>, SPCK, 2003, p. 92
2. Lewis, C.S., <u>Mere Christianity</u>, Fount, 1978, p.121-2
3. Julian of Norwich, <u>Revelations of Divine Love</u>, Penguin Classics 1966, p. 161
4. Ulanov, Ann and Barry, <u>Primary Speech, a Psychology of Prayer</u>, John Knox press, 1982. p.102
5. ibid., p.105
6. Ward, J. Neville, <u>The Use of Praying</u>, Epworth. 1978. p.99
7. ibid., p.100
8. Ulanov, op. cit., p.101
9. Valles, Carlos, <u>Mastering Sadhana</u>, Fount 1991, p. 83f.
10. Baelz, Peter, <u>Prayer and Providence</u>, SCM, 1968, p.34
11. Dossey, Larry, <u>Healing Words</u>, Harper San Francisco, 1993
12. Baelz, op. cit, p.30
13. ibid., p.49
14. Ryrie, Alexander, <u>Wonderful Exchange</u>, an exploration of silent prayer, Canterbury Press, 1989, p.44
15. ibid., p.84
16. Pritchard, op. cit. p.33
17. Ryrie, op. cit., p.83
18. Ward, op. cit., p.88
19. Pritchard, op. cit. p.33
20. Ulanov, op. cit. p.17

# Chapter 4
## Just Being

How many times do we hear those words from school teachers – 'be quiet' or simply 'stop talking'. I wonder whether God would like to use those words as well. God must get very tired of our ceaseless chatter.

Z: Imagine going to your doctor, talking for ten minutes and then walking out!

Yes. If prayer is, in any sense, a conversation then at least for some of the time we have to be silent otherwise a dialogue has not taken place. Bonhoeffer wrote years ago that 'the Word comes not to the chatterer but to him who holds his tongue'. (1) and goes on to write about the ministry of holding one's tongue. (2) This latter reference is in the context of how we speak about other people and making the point that it is often better to remain silent and it is certainly better than speaking words of judgement or unkind criticism. The idea of holding one's tongue, though, appeals to me when praying. Words are concepts but silent contemplation is reaching God without any concepts.

Prayer, for me, is not calling upon God to bring to God's

attention a situation that he already knows about. It is opening oneself up in the presence of God to the myriad number of possibilities that could happen and the possibility of discerning one's role in a future course of action. 'Prayer is not talking to God *but being with him*. Prayer is an awareness of being loved.' (3) For this to happen I think that we have to be silent in the presence of God rather than present him with a tirade of words. We are therefore, not thinking about anything but concentrating on the presence of God. Of course, it has to be said that different temperaments enjoy different kinds of prayer. Ruth Fowke has written about this in her book 'Personality and Prayer'. (4)

Z: I'm all for that. Some people are even afraid of clowns although I can't imagine why.

My personal preference is to use words sometimes but most of the time to sit in total silence. I tend not to be very organised and have always found it difficult using anything like a daily office.

Z: I thought people went to work in an office.

Sorry Zeno. I've used a bit of jargon. The daily office in this context is a set of prayers and bible readings that some clergy use every day as part of their spiritual discipline. Some people like to pray whilst they are doing something else. For me, personally, God often speaks when I am out jogging.

Z: You going jogging? I've seen more movement in a beached whale.
Does God tell you to run a bit faster?

Not at all Zeno. God is far more encouraging and says things like, 'you are doing well', 'keep going you are nearly there', 'take it easy, don't be too hard on yourself'.

God does not pour scorn on our pathetic attempts but accepts us as we are and so the relationship becomes one in which we can grow and develop. Anyway, to get back to the point, the very thought of jogging is for some anathema and so they might pray as they take the dog for a walk, do some gardening or some ironing.

Z: What about those who say they can't pray at all?

I agree that is a very real problem. There is a feeling around that for prayer to be legitimate it has to be framed with special, holy words. Nothing could be further from the truth. There is a lovely example of praying in a book called 'From the bottom of the pond'. (5) A woman complains that she just can't pray but on closer inspection she is clearly praying as she washes the dishes and gazes at the view from her kitchen window. Hundreds of years ago, Brother Lawrence wrote about practising the presence of God as he worked in the monastery kitchen. However, I want to concentrate here on just being silent, ostensibly doing nothing.

Z: Isn't there a Zen saying: Sitting quietly, doing nothing, Spring comes and the grass grows by itself?

That's right. I wonder where you came across that. Ann Lewin has recently written the following

You do not have to look for anything,
Just look.
You do not have to listen for
Specific sounds,

Just listen.
You do not have to accomplish anything,
Just be.

And in the looking
And the listening
And the being,
Find
Me. (6)

Z: I read somewhere the following; I don't say anything to God. I just sit there and look at him and let him look at me. (7) This is all very well but just sitting there being quiet I find quite difficult. Anyway, aren't there different kinds of silence?

There are certainly different kinds of silence. There is the embarrassed silence when nobody knows what to say. There is the angry silence when, for example, a husband cannot find the words to express himself, but the silence is palpable. There is the silence of rejection, the cold shoulder. There is the wall of silence when the police, attempting to find a witness, are met by nil response. There is the silence of acquiescence or complicity, that is, by saying nothing we are agreeing to something whether we approve of it or not. There is the silence of simply not knowing what to say. There is the comfortable silence when two friends or partners are comfortable in each other's presence. There is the silence of lovers.

Z: Are you getting back to sex again?

Can you be quiet just for once? There is the silence of shock or amazement when, perhaps, we suddenly come across a wonderful view and words are not sufficient to describe the breathtaking sensation, we are absolutely speechless. There is the silence of solitary confinement when silence is used by captors as a weapon to break down resistance. There is the silence of thanksgiving each year on Remembrance Day when two minutes can seem like an eternity. I am sure there are other kinds of silence but our concern here is with our silence before God and that silence may well include some of those listed above.

Z: I can remember trying to do something funny and nobody laughed. The silence was deafening!

I have written elsewhere about my own experience of silence and I have no doubt whatsoever that it saved my spiritual bacon. The opportunity to let go of all the usual paraphernalia of everyday life – music, television, post, knocks on the door, telephone calls, emails, family distractions, reading – allowed room for God to speak. (8)

Z: And did God speak?

Without a doubt. At the start of a thirty day silent retreat I really, really struggled with so much silence. On the first day I thought that the chances of making it through the whole thirty days were very slim. Then I heard from my spiritual director words of advice, which I had heard before but which now suddenly were filled with new meaning, 'take it a day at a time'. In actual fact, I took it an hour at a time and with that came the realisation that God is always in the present moment. Not in the past or the future but in the here and now and therefore to find God one has to concentrate on what is happening here and now. Moreover, God provides strength only for the present. In the Lord's prayer, we say 'Give us this day our daily bread'. The children of Israel during their forty years wandering in the wilderness were supplied with mystical bread called manna but if they tried to store it up for more than one day, it became mouldy. Matthew writes, 'So do not worry about tomorrow, for tomorrow brings worries of its own. Today's trouble is enough for today'. (Matthew 6:34)

Of course, some will argue that I am living in cloud cuckoo land. The voice I heard was simply my own speaking to myself. All I can say is that it didn't feel like that. I know when I'm talking to my self.

Z: You soon get bored listening to yourself.

One of the problems is that we are simply not used to silence and so we fear we will be overwhelmed. In the main, there is a fear of silence and so we tend to rebel against it. We may have to face some unpleasant things about ourselves that we have been trying to avoid. The easy way out is to go for the background music or constant television, a ceaseless chatter that fools us into thinking we are not alone and that prevents us from facing our inner demons. Much better to 'drown' out the silence with noise of any description otherwise disturbing questions may arise. Anyway it is better to give the impression of actually doing something rather than, apparently, sitting and doing nothing.

Another thing is that silence can be unpredictable. One day I may be perfectly content to go for a solitary walk or sit in my room with a book and cup of coffee completely alone and feel totally at ease. Another day I may be clamouring to talk to someone or longing for the phone to ring, if only to break the silence. In church I may just be tired of all the singing and the readings and the sermon, in short, tired of all the words.

I long for a bit of peace and quiet so that I can meditate and reflect on my own. On another occasion I may just want the preacher to say a bit more about a particular subject or long to sing something more to express my feelings.

Silence is also unpredictable in the sense of whether God will reveal anything or not. Will God speak or not? How will I know it is God? What will actually happen? There is no easy answer to these questions because one thing is for sure, we cannot control God. It is entirely up to God whether there is self disclosure or not. Before pursuing these questions let us look at some of the early influences within the Christian tradition.

In the Old Testament there is the text 'in quietness and trust shall be your strength'. ( Is 30:15) but there is also the well known verse in psalm 46. Amidst all the noise and tumult of war and associated calamities the psalmist closes with the verse 'be still, and know that I am God'. (psalm 46: 10) The Jerusalem bible has, 'pause a while and know that I am God'. The old Latin version has, 'empty yourself and know that I am God'. This notion of emptying ourselves is much more helpful because there is no room for God until we are empty. A person once went to a guru for advice about how to find God. The guru poured out a cup of coffee and kept pouring even when the cup was full. This is an acted out example of the truism that there is no room for anything, let alone God, when we are full. The person who was seeking advice was too busy to take heed of what the guru had to say.

Z: Exactly the same thing happens when I am packing my case full of effects. I always want to pack in more than the case will hold. For a start I have lots of different noses and hats.

Another biblical example is the story of the prophet Elijah. He feared what Queen Jezebel would do to him after her prophets had been humiliated by Elijah on Mount Carmel. He fled into the wilderness and sat down under a 'solitary broom tree' and asked that God might take away his life. (1 Kings 19: 4) He then travelled for forty days and nights until he came across a cave on Mount Sinai where he spent the night. It was here that Elijah heard the voice of God, not in a great wind, nor in an earthquake or a fire but in 'a sound of sheer silence'. (1 Kings 19: 12) Of course, four centuries earlier Moses had met God on this very mountain but his journey had begun when he had heard God speaking to him through the burning bush in the desert. God spoke to these two figures of Jewish history when they were on their own in silence in the desert.

Z: The desert seems to be very important but I don't fancy going there at all.

I agree that the desert can be a frightening, empty, God forsaken place but it is really a symbol of dryness. To that extent the desert is not a place at all, not an external location but a place within all of us. We experience it when we feel spiritually dry, arid and empty.

This desert, or wilderness, tradition was taken up in the New Testament by John the Baptist, the last in a long line of prophets. 'The child grew and became strong in spirit; and he was in the wilderness until the day he appeared publicly to Israel.' (Luke 1:80) In Mark's gospel we read it was in the wilderness that John proclaimed his message of a baptism of repentance. (Mark 1:1ff) The importance of silence and the solitude of the wilderness were experienced by Jesus, himself, when he spent forty days there and overcame various temptations. There, in the wilderness, he discovered his identity, his hidden resolve and his vocation. Moreover, the short life of Jesus was not completely bound up with teaching, healing, performing miracles and the like. There are many references to him wanting to be alone to pray, often up a mountain. The life of Jesus was not one of ceaseless busyness without respite. He seemed to sense the need to spend time with God, away from the crowds and even from the disciples. How can you bring others close to God if you are not close to God yourself and for this, time needs to be given in order to develop the relationship? 'In the morning, while it was still very dark, he got up and went out to a deserted place, and there he prayed. And Simon and his companions hunted for him.' (Mark 1: 35-36) 'Now during those days he went out to the mountain to pray, and he spent the night in prayer to God.' (Luke 6:12) In the garden of Gethsemane Jesus prayed alone.

No wonder that the early monks saw in Jesus their example and prototype for living a solitary life. 'The real test for generations of monks and nuns has been to embrace solitude as a locus for communion with and contemplation of God, rather than as a supposed escape from human suffering or the complications inherent in human relations. So the monastic heart has fixed its gaze on Jesus in his solitariness, to transform a contemplative moment in life into a contemplative movement of life, and to join its own contemplative gaze with that of Jesus in solitary contemplative union with the Father.' (9)

This monastic tradition began with the desert fathers and mothers, people who deliberately chose to live lives of great hardship and privation in the hostile environs of the deserts of Egypt. The movement was partly a reaction to what happened to Christianity after 312 AD when Emperor

Constantine converted to Christianity. The problem was how to maintain the values of the Kingdom which Jesus had proclaimed within a society that, at least, nominally, had become Christian. Christians no longer needed to live in secrecy; martyrdom ceased to be an issue; people were no longer required to worship idols, including the Emperor, and pacifism was no longer thought to be viable because the army was seen to be defending Christian values. In brief, Christianity was no longer an illegal or minority movement. One reaction to all this was to build churches and cathedrals and develop the life of the church within the towns and cities. The other reaction was to live a purer, more ascetic life based on Kingdom values in isolated monasteries and communities in the desert. In order to avoid the distractions of the big cities like Alexandria, they escaped into the desert. It was felt that in the sandy wastes, people could devote themselves entirely to the business of giving themselves to God without unnecessary things getting in the way.

They were able to develop a systematic rhythm to each day which, naturally, included times of prayer.

Z: I think most people could 'be' in a monastery and pray in silence but the reality is that most people in the 'real' world lead busy lives often punctuated with lots of noise from families and elsewhere.

I agree that it is much harder to be quiet when there are children around but I am reminded of Susannah Wesley, the wife of John Wesley. She had a large family but when she wanted to pray she simply put a towel over her head and the family knew they had to be quiet.

Z: I think health and safety experts might have something to say about that today!

An idea that I find helpful is taken from the Buddhist tradition and is called 'mindfulness'. This is to know what is going on within and around us at any moment in time. It is to practise the awareness of being in the present moment rather than being lost in the past or overcome with thoughts about the future. When the Buddha was asked, "Sir, what do you and your monks practice?" He replied, "We sit, we walk, and we eat." The questioner continued, "But sir, everyone sits, walks, and eats." and the Buddha told him, "When we walk, we *know* we are walking, when we *sit*, we know we are sitting, when we *eat*, we know we are eating." (10) I think this is what St. Paul had in mind then he exhorts his readers to 'pray without ceasing'. (1Thess. 5:17) He is not asking that we are always on our knees talking to God but that we lead our lives in a prayerful or mindful kind of way.

Z: I noted that when you were walking over some icy footpaths the other day, you had to be very mindful.

I certainly did. It's a bit like jogging…

Z: 'erewigoagain!

…all I was going to say is that you have to keep focussed on the next step. There is a need to have a longer view as well but if you, literally, don't look where you are going it is easy to trip up and fall.

Z: I guess the older you get the easier it is to fall and therefore the more important it is to keep focussed and concentrate.

You certainly do but mindfulness is something younger people could cultivate as well. Perhaps a more familiar word than mindfulness is awareness. A mobile phone is no good unless it is switched on. Then messages can be received from more or less anywhere. The question for me is can I, as a person, be switched on? In all honesty a lot of the time I am not switched on. It is all too easy to go around with ones eyes metaphorically closed to the world around. I love to watch people on a London tube train. Everybody is in their own world trying not to make eye contact with anybody, or not daring to, They have their eyes down, immersed in a book or the morning paper or maybe their eyes are shut as they listen to their i-pod.

Earth's crammed with heaven and every common bush afire with God
But only he who sees takes off his shoes.
The rest sit round it and pluck blackberries. (11)

Z: I don't think you see many blackberries on the London tube train!

Even in church there can sometimes be very little awareness of God, or indeed, of each other. It is possible to sit next to somebody for a whole hour and there be no meaningful contact at all.

Z: That's why I try to get people to laugh. At least it breaks down some barriers and brings people together. Just throw a balloon into a group of people and see what happens!

Anthony de Mello distinguishes between knowledge and awareness. We can have knowledge about something yet it makes very little impact on our way of life.

Z: You mean like climate change that you mentioned earlier?

We all know about the problem but don't take any action or we think it won't affect us.

Yes, that's it exactly. You can be quite bright sometimes Zeno. De Mello uses another example. A person can know that tobacco kills people but just carries on smoking. In fact he jokes about it. "Just look at the ancient Egyptians; they're all dead and none of them smoked." Then one day he goes to hospital and discovers he has got two patches on his lungs. He is told by the specialist that it could be cancer. He never touched another cigarette after that. 'Before he *knew* it would kill him; now, he was *aware* it could kill him.' (12)

One of the things that deaden awareness is familiarity. In one sense it is good to be familiar but there is a very great danger that we take things for granted. A good antidote is to listen to children.

Z: Why?

Precisely for that reason. They are always asking the question 'why'. If you want to be kept on your toes in the church, or any other group, including family, listen to a child asking why. They oblige you to give a reason for a particular ritual or course of action that you are engaged in.

Z: You mean like 'why do you go to Church?' 'Why do people worship?' 'Why do you never clean your car?' 'Why do you always have to get drunk?'

Well that's a mixed bag of examples but you are right! However, I fear we have diverged a bit from my main point which is the importance of being silent before God. I think that when we can simply 'be' before God then there is a greater possibility of heightening our awareness and our mindfulness. This does not have to happen in a monastery but it can happen anywhere. Maybe one can find half an hour everyday, or an hour every week, or one can practise this kind of meditation whilst commuting on the train into work. Somehow whilst the brain is engaged in an activity which doesn't demand much concentration, it allows a deeper level of consciousness to be reached. I find it helpful to be doing something as well.

Z: I hope you are not going to talk about jogging again.

Not at all, although I could! It can happen whilst I am watching the television. The programme is usually so boring I mentally switch off and go to another internal place.

Z: You mean you have forty winks?

I admit that sometimes I do drop off but at other times I am 'meditating' inside whilst being completely oblivious to what is on the box. In the main, though, it is more helpful to meditate in a more systematic way. 'Those who go in for it do so not because it is a pleasant and attractive option, but because they feel they can do no other; they have an inner urge, and they have no choice. In the prayer of silence they engage with a God whom they cannot grasp but from whom they cannot escape; who will not show himself but whom they cannot avoid; who will not take them fully to himself but who will not let them go; who will not be wholly present but who will not go away. It is a task in which progress cannot be measured, and whose goal seems always beyond us; an investment with no quick return. It is undertaken not only by saints or mystics, but by ordinary people who are not especially good or holy or prayerful, who feel to the end that they are not very at good at it, and may frequently wonder why they are doing it at all.' (13)

Z: Phew; that was a long quotation.

My apologies, but Ryrie does say just what I wanted to say. There is a hint in the quote, and you have mentioned it before, how difficult this kind of prayer is, not just because of the nature of silence itself but also because of the distractions. There are too many distractions which is precisely why the monastic tradition began. However, there are not only the external distractions – baby crying, television, traffic outside, even a clock ticking – but the internal ones. Every time I try to concentrate and focus on God, thoughts come flooding into my mind and the elusive moment disappears. The problem of distractions can be overcome by learning to concentrate on the present. Our minds like to keep busy and so we think about what has happened, we reminisce, we remember. All too easily we think about the future and sometimes we are anxious and fearful about what may or may not happen. In a sense we are too busy living to think about Life. Life in its fullness is in the here and now. The present is all we have and the present is precisely where God can be found. This has been called the sacrament of the present moment. However, with our plans for the future and our memories of the past the present moment is squeezed out. As Charles Wesley wrote, 'the fugitive moment refuses to stay'. (14)

Z: If my memory is right I think there is another line in that very same hymn. 'And never stand still till the Master appear.'

You are right Zeno. Wesley is not a good example for quiet contemplation. He rode through the country on horseback to preach and in a single day he would ride seventy miles and preach three sermons. He learned to ride with a slack reign so that he could read or write while in the saddle. In his letters he wrote 'leisure and I have now taken leave of one another – I propose to be busy as long as a live'.

Z: It's a wonder he had any time to pray at all.

Well, he was certainly a man of prayer. It's just that he never wanted to waste time. In his old age he wrote: 'Lord, let me not live to be useless.' There seems to have been a 'driven-ness' about Wesley that I find difficult to come to terms with. I find it more helpful to think of God as inviting rather than driving.

Z: That helps me for sure. Slaves are driven and I certainnly don't want to be a slave.

Good, but let's get back to prayer. Here are some suggestions for staying in the present moment although, at the end of the day, prayer is not about some esoteric technique but about deepening one's relationship with God.

My personal preference is to concentrate on my breathing, that is, breathing quite normally but whenever I wander off and think of something else I return to concentrate on my breathing. There is no need to change your normal breathing pattern. Simply be aware of your breathing in and your breathing out.

Z: That is an excellent way of falling asleep!

At other times I lose my head by going into my senses. I become aware of the seat I am sitting on, the floor on which my feet rest, any aches and pains in my body and so on. Concentrating on an ache is a wonderful way of coming into the present moment! All else is forgotten. Some people start with their feet, squeezing and relaxing various muscles until they finish somewhere round their head and shoulders.

Other people find it helpful to give their brain something to do whilst engaged in silent prayer. Repeating a phrase or mantra over and over again, for example, 'Lord have mercy', or 'come Lord Jesus'. John Main writes about the use of a mantra. 'Through the continual silent repetition of a prayer phrase or mantra, the meditator turns away from the imagination and self-consciousness towards an interior silence where God is discovered not in the illusion of reality but in the reality of faith.' (15) It doesn't really matter what the phrase is. Another suggestion is to use a focus – a candle, a picture, an icon – as a way of staying concentrated. There isn't one and only one way to pray! Others prefer to concentrate on a biblical passage. Some favour a cerebral approach whilst others are more spontaneous and speak from the heart.

These are only suggestions. Each of us has to find out which method is more helpful for a prayerful state of mind. There is nothing prescriptive but it sometimes helps to have a change, especially if your prayer life has become very dry. Of course, if a particular thought is persistent then it may well be that God is trying to tell you something and it therefore needs to be followed up. It can help to have a piece of paper to hand to scribble down any random thoughts you have like the need to buy a birthday card for somebody.

Z: Even if by some stroke of luck I manage to keep quiet and somehow get in touch with the presence of God I think it could be argued that I have simply escaped from the world into some cosy, comfortable state of being.

I have no doubt at all that being with God is not always comfortable. It is true that God can comfort the afflicted but the opposite is also true. God very much afflicts the comfortable, at least, if we are listening! We will turn to the problem of escapism, which I agree is very real, in the next chapter but first I wanted to look at the question of silence in worship.

Many years ago, when I was just beginning as a preacher, during one of my very first church services, I was feeling very radical and decided to have a few moments of silent prayer. After what must have only been a couple of minutes I distinctly heard someone in the congregation whisper 'has he gone to sleep?'

Z: That's the difference between an audience and a congregation. An audience listens. (16)

I hope it is obvious by now that listening is very important. A few days ago I was having some fun with my two year old granddaughter. 'Where's your nose?' I asked.
She duly pointed to her nose. She was able to do this with various points of her face and body. Through the listening she understood long before she was able to put anything into words.

Z: Ah yes. We have two ears but only one mouth. It is doubly more important to listen.

Precisely. Since retiring I have found myself, more often than not, sitting in a pew rather than standing at the front leading an act of worship and that has entailed a great deal of listening. It has been a steep learning curve which has given me, for various reasons, a completely different perspective. The overall impression is that worship comes over as a torrent of words. This is especially difficult to come to terms with when it is realised that not only do we live in a visual culture, but we are also dominated by sound bites. I think it stretches the imagination to think that young people indeed, most people, can concentrate on a sermon that lasts for twenty minutes. Moreover, prayers, especially if they are read, need time to be digested.

'Church worship is enriched when there are pauses for reflection between words and music because our prayers and statements of faith need room to breath. Imagine a book that had no margins, so that every page was completely covered with text, or an art gallery where all the pictures were crowded onto a single wall.' (17) Space is needed between the words. Space to let God in. Space to allow for a sense of awe and mystery. Space to draw breath and to reflect otherwise there is a danger of severe verbal indigestion.

Z: Perhaps preachers could issue everybody with an indigestion tablet to take before the sermon.

That would certainly have an effect but misses the point. With regard to sermons, at best, people go away and think about them but carry on as normal. Intellectual inquiry does not lead a person to an awareness of God. Listening to a sermon does not usually bring about an inner change. In the main congregations live their lives as they did before. Inner change begins to happen when we appropriate an idea or experience at a deeper level of our being than in our heads. It is like giving people advice. The advice can be accepted with the head but if it is not taken on board at a much deeper lever the advice will not be followed. Change happens when an idea is 'taken on board', when an idea, or concept, is internalised into the heart. A question can be discussed endlessly but it will not of itself effect change until there is a change in the heart. The head recognises that God is a given but it is the heart that opens itself to God's presence.

Silence is a way into the heart. Silence is a gift and a friend. It is not just a question of being quiet but it is alerting one's sense to the presence of God. This is mindfulness or awareness. God is often crowded out by our words and liturgy. Too often the church is a structure of tight rules, some of which are spoken and others are assumed. For God to break through it may be necessary to break the rules.

Z: I'm all for that! What a great idea.

For me, the acid test to any act of worship is; has God been encountered? Have I been helped or hindered in this worship? Hymns or songs have been sung, prayers have been said, or read, a sermon has been preached, often read, but there has been no sense of being in touch with 'the wholly other.' Some years ago my wife and I were abroad on holiday and we attended an English speaking church for their Sunday service. After the service, which was totally traditional, we visited a nearby museum. As one might expect, this was full of ancient artefacts, many of them about religious deities that were worshipped long before Christianity came onto the scene. In fact, they predated Stonehenge. The fascinating thing is that both my wife and I experienced a far great feeling of transcendence in the museum that we had in the church service! There was a great feeling of being in touch with something intangible, mysterious, and deeply spiritual.

Not only is God very often not encountered but also there is a reluctance to encounter each other. My experience of attending church as a visitor is that someone usually offers a hand shake and word of welcome on entering but that is as far as it goes. Other people might offer a smile and a 'good morning' but there is rarely a significant conversation and certainly no conversation about God or anything spiritual. I have often sat next to people who have offered no conversation at all.

Z: Perhaps it's your fault. You need to take the first step and not just wait for others to do all the work.

I can't imagine that strangers in an early Christian community would have been treated so blandly. They would have been welcomed, I'm sure, with great enthusiasm and enjoyed shared hospitality round a meal table. Faith stories would have been exchanged and communication at depth would have taken place. People today are far more reticent and so the idea of Christian fellowship has lost a lot of its former, rich meaning. When people only meet at a superficial level it is far removed from the true meaning of fellowship.

Z: Ah yes, the good old days!!

Many times I also feel undernourished having attended a church service. I have met other people who feel the same. Maybe this is why people are leaving the church. They are finding it no longer satisfies their spiritual hunger.

Z: Do you remember on one occasion we were both in church for a communion service and instead of small pieces of bread or dry wafers there was a great big loaf of bread?

Yes. It was an excellent example of the generosity of God. I was so surprised I couldn't help smiling. The love of God knows no barriers or limitations but,

'Religion sets limitations, and lures the seeker into dealing with issues which seem to belong to the perpetuation of the system rather than the growth of the person.' (18) The result is that there is more concern with filling the pews rather than feeding the people.

Of course, we cannot control the presence of God or decide how or when God is encountered. It is not we who encounter God, but God who encounters us. Our part is to lay ourselves open to this encounter. More often than not, this is not a matter of saying or doing anything, but of BEING – simply being who and what we are in the presence of God. By being in silence in this way we put ourselves in a position to encounter God. God is not known through our rational minds, although they can help our understanding, but through an encounter, an I-thou relationship in which we stand before God in the depth of our hearts and encounter God as a personal presence. (19)

## **Points to ponder:**

1. How do you feel when you are silent?

2. Which kind of silence are you most familiar with?

3. On Remembrance Sunday, there is usually two minutes silence? How does it feel?

4. Ponder on the times in your life when you have been aware of God's presence? What was that like for you?

5. When do you experience a tension within you between the need to be doing something and the need to be still? Where does that tension come from?

## Meditation:

Breathing in, I calm my body.
Breathing out, I smile.
Dwelling in the present moment,
I know this is a wonderful moment. (20)

## References

1. Bonhoeffer, Dietrich, Life Together, SCM, 1954, p.59
2. ibid., p.70
3. McKenty, Neil, In The Stillness Dancing, The Journey of John Main, DLT, 1987, p.88
4. Fowke, Ruth, Personality and Prayer, Eagle, 1997: see also, Osborn, Lawrence & Diana, God's Diverse People, Daybreak, 1991 also, Goldsmith, Malcolm & Wharton, Martin, Knowing Me Knowing You, SPCK, 1993
5. Small, Simon, From the Bottom of the Pond, O Books, 2008, p. 11-12
6. Lewin, Ann, Watching for the Kingfisher, Inspire, 2004, p.16
7. Law, Philip, Secrets of Prayer, Lion, 1999, p. 1
8. Rothwell, Malcolm, Journeying with God, Epworth, 2001
9. Belisle, Peter-Damian, The Language of Silence, DLT, 2003, p. 38

10. Hanh, Thich Nhat, <u>Living Buddha, Living Christ</u>, Rider, 1995, p. 14

11. Browning, Elizabeth Barrett, <u>Aurora Leigh</u>, Book vii, Line 820

12. de Mello, Anthony, <u>Awareness</u>, Fount, 1990, p. 168

13. Ryrie, Alexander, <u>Wonderful Exchange</u>, Canterbury, 2003, p.3

14. <u>Hymns and Psalms</u>, 354

15. see McKenty, op. cit., p.85

16. Watts, Murray, <u>Preachers at Large</u>, Monarch, 1999, p.68

17. Ashwin, Angela, <u>Faith in the Fool</u>, DLT, 2009, p.128

18. Ó Murchú, Diarmuid, <u>Reclaiming Spirituality</u>, Gill & Macmillan, 1997, p.31

19. Note: Some say that the idea of a covenant relationship between God and his people is central to both Old and New Testaments but Faber, building on the work of Terrien, argues that the idea of presence is more important. 'The idea of covenant is secondary to the experience of God's presence'. (\*\*) God's presence is often very elusive but we can experience it, whereas a covenant, although it expresses a relationship between God and humankind, cannot be experienced in the same way. Some might say that it cannot be experienced at all.

    \*\* Faber, Heije, <u>Above the Treeline</u>, SCM, 1988, p.7

20. Hanh, op. cit., p.16

# Chapter 5

## BEING JUST OR SHEER ESCAPISM

Z: I think that sometimes people disappear on a retreat or into a time of contemplation so they can escape into their own little world. For me that is not an option. The action is 'out there', not in some private cocoon that you have created to protect yourself. I am not into holy huddles at all.

Let me put you right on that one Zeno. There are plenty of examples in the New Testament where Jesus goes off on his own to pray. Furthermore he encouraged people to pray in the quietness of their own rooms. (Matt 6:6)

Z: I don't dispute that. It is more the issue of contemplation which suggests the image of people gazing intently at their own navel.

I'm sure that is the last thing Jesus had in mind. Navel gazing is not an option for Christians. Contemplation has been described as 'a long loving look at the real'. (1) If you take a long loving look at something – a child playing, a rose in full bloom, the sun setting, a bird hovering in the sky, your partner, an appetising meal – then that is contemplation. You may well ask what is real.

Z: You took the words out of my mouth!

Reality is watching someone enjoy an ice cream, or listening to a Beethoven concerto.

Z: Or a pop song?

Yes indeed. I recently went to a concert of Queen music. It was wonderful. Contemplation is gazing at a mountain stream, not analysing it into its component parts, $H_2O$. Similarly, one can gaze at the cross of Jesus but again analysing is not the same as contemplating. To gaze on the mystery and to wonder is far more powerful than trying to make sense of all the theories of the atonement.

Z: I'm glad you are not going to go into all those. Too many long words for me! Anyway I think most of them miss the mark. Surely Jesus was crucified because of the jealousies and fears of the religious leaders of that time. People took themselves far too seriously, as they do now, and as a result, a great injustice was done.

I think you are right but, of course, the early followers of Jesus had to try and make sense of his horrific death. A few days earlier they had been his devoted followers and then, suddenly, the life was literally hammered out of him. It is exactly the same today. If somebody we love dies suddenly we have to try and make sense of it. We search for a meaning in order to alleviate our shock and despair. There may be a spiritual meaning like all things work together for good for those who love God, or, it must have been God's will. People say things like, once your number is up there is nothing you can do, or, it was his fault for driving too fast. The problem is that as soon as we start to find explanations the mystery is lost. Some would argue that life is not a problem to be solved but a mystery to be explored.

Z: When you say mystery do you mean where do socks go when they enter the washing machine? or what do women have in their hand bags?

Those are problems that can be solved, like an Agatha Christie whodunit. Put Hercule Poirot or Miss Marple on the case, the culprit is eventually found and the mystery solved. I mean mystery in the sense of wonder, not in the sense of a problem that can be solved. Incidentally, although we live in a predominantly scientific culture which makes belief in God difficult, as we have seen, I think that science along with religion has some roots in this idea of wonder.

Z: This is all very well. I can gaze with wonder at a red nose as much as anybody else but what about things which aren't so funny and not at all enjoyable.

I'm afraid that reality very much includes the things you have in mind, a homeless person dying in a shop door way, a child soldier in Somalia, a Palestinian family forcibly evicted from their home, a little baby dying of Aids, a child with distended belly longing for water and a morsel of food, a soldier writhing in pain with shrapnel, a father distraught because his son has been knifed in a mugging – the list is endless. Real is not always beautiful. Far from it. But notice that the original definition included the word 'loving'. Contemplation is a long *loving* look at the real.

Z: In all honesty I find I want to turn away from some of the scenes you have described. I wouldn't want to take a long look. The thought of a *long* look at them is not something I relish. You many be interested to know that one of my ancestors, Grimaldi, had a very difficult life. His first wife died, his son predeceased him and then his second wife died. Through it all he remained a very famous clown although he suffered from depression.

There is a natural human tendency to turn away or to deny the pain. Once we start contemplating or gazing at somebody or a situation with love then we come close to looking with the eyes of Jesus, who is the personification of love. The real world is full of pain and suffering yet, 'the real I contemplate must end in compassion, and compassion that mimics Christ is a synonym for love'. (2)

Z: This is all very well but what if the pain is too great.

It is a sexist comment but men, in general, are not as good as women at dealing with pain. Remember at the crucifixion the women stayed to watch but the men were nowhere to be seen! We can also escape in a variety of ways. It is much easier for a church meeting to discuss the colour of the church toilets than search for ways of becoming involved in the community.

Z: That reminds me of another of Anthony de Mello's stories which takes place in the month of October 1917, the very month that the Russian Revolution was born.

'The story goes that that very month the Russian Church was assembled in council. A passionate debate was in progress about the colour of the surplice to be used in liturgical functions. Some insisted vehemently that it had to be white. Others, with equal vehemence, that it had to be purple.' (3) De Mello comments 'coming to grips with a revolution is more of a bother than organising a liturgy. I'd rather say my prayers than get involved in neighbourhood disputes'.

That is a perfect illustration of how easy it is to turn inwards and think about yourself and your own little world rather than issues of real importance. Simon Bailey was an Anglican priest who was diagnosed HIV positive and eventually died of Aids. From that context of struggle and suffering he wrote, 'we have let these things, - justice and prayer, spirituality and politics- get impossibly separated'. (4) We talk of personal spirituality and so there is a danger of spirituality becoming 'the subtlest and most devious of the Thatcherite privatisations'. (5) How can I be at peace within when my Christian brothers and sisters are dying for lack of nourishment? How can I truly enjoy all the comforts I have when other people live in abject poverty?

Z: I often get the feeling that the problems are so large there is nothing that little old me can do.

As somebody once said, for evil to prosper all that is needed is for good people to do nothing. Granted individuals often cannot do very much, and they certainly cannot do everything, but there is the possibility of doing something and doing that something well. There is the story of someone walking along a beach in Australia and he noticed a man taking the trouble to throw marooned star fish back into the sea. 'Why bother, you aren't going to make any difference'. The man replied, 'I've made a difference to that one.'

I remember demonstrating in London, along with about

a million other people, against a possible invasion of Iraq. As a matter of interest, I actually walked beside two young people who had taken the trouble to travel down from North Yorkshire. History records that this massive demonstration made no difference to the intentions of Blair and Bush. The invasion duly took place. However, I felt as though I had done something tangible. On a more positive note demonstrations for a more equitable distribution of the world's wealth and for fairer trade agreements have certainly had an effect in shaping government policy.

Prayer is not an escape. Just as food empowers us and gives us energy, so does prayer. Being still and available for God is not an escape from the world. Leech writes, 'The struggle for justice embraces both inward discipline and outward activity. What is spirituality? It surely only has a depth that is continuous with the rest of our lives if it reckons with, confronts face to face, rather than trying to escape, oppression and prejudice, pain and violence, recession and poverty, failure, inadequacy, emptiness and fear. 'Spirituality' and 'spiritual life' are not religious departments, walled-off areas of life. Rather the spiritual life is the life of the whole person directed towards God'. (6) God is in the everyday – in all things. That is one of the great insights of Ignatian spirituality. If at one moment you feel like being spiritual, what do you feel like in the next moment? For an authentic spirituality there must be continuity through all the activities of our lives.

Z: So we need to be like sticks of rock with the word 'spirituality' going all the way through from top to bottom, not just touching bits here and there.

Exactly. Maybe it is buying the Big Issue and having a chat

with the vendor instead of rushing past with a guilty feeling. Even as we stand at the supermarket check out, or wait in the traffic jam, our spirituality needs to be present.

Z: Well I know for a fact that your spirituality isn't always present, especially at the supermarket check out. You are just too impatient.

I know that only too well. I disappoint myself more often than not. My great regret is that I am not always giving a long loving look at the real and so the result is that people don't experience God through me.

Z: Not to worry. It's better than being perfect! If you were perfect there wouldn't be another step to take. You would have arrived. Anyway I thought only Jesus was perfect.

I'm not sure about that word perfect but I do think that Jesus is authentic. As J.B. Philips said many years ago, there is the ring of truth about him. That is one of the things that attracts me to him. There is continuity in his life. His actions match his words. 'Be concerned above everything else with the Kingdom of God and with what he requires of you.' (Matt. 6: 33 TEV) So often there is a tendency to stop at the first phrase, the Kingdom of God, and not go any further but both phrases have to be held in tension. It is important to work out what God requires of us in any given situation. Charles Elliott wrote a few years ago, 'there can be no spirituality without action'. (7)

There is the oft quoted verse in the letter of James, 'So faith by itself, if it has no works, is dead'. (James 2:17) Faith of itself is not sufficient. Jesus says exactly the same. He challenges people not only to hear his words but also to act upon them.

The people who act on them will be like 'a wise man who built his house upon rock'. (Matt. 7: 24) Everyone who does not act upon the words of Jesus is like a 'foolish man who built his house upon sand'. (Matt. 7: 26)

Z: Haven't some people done this quite literally in Dubai?

Yes they have, and if they don't fall literally in the sand they are being engulfed in a stream of huge debts. Jesus says that one cannot simply say Lord, Lord, in the hope of entering the Kingdom of Heaven but only those 'who do the will of my Father in heaven'. (Matt. 7.21) In the fourth gospel are the words, 'the one who believes in me will also do the works that I do', (John 14: 12) and in the first letter of John there is the thought that if you don't love your brothers and sisters who you can see, how can you love God who you can't see. (1 John 4: 20). 'Let us love, not in word or speech, but in truth and action'. (1 John 3:18) We see that Jesus not only preaches about love and doing good to others but bears it out in his life. For those who would be his followers the message is clear. They also have to live lives of love.

Z: I think you are beginning to make your point. Jesus puts his money where is mouth is. However, you seem to be implying that Christian people are not involved in 'good deeds'.

That would not be fair at all. I have known many people through my life who have been members of the church and who have been the salt of the earth. They have gone out of their way to care for other people, often under most difficult circumstances. I remember Rachel who was confined to her own home but nevertheless wrote letters to church members who were in hospital even if she didn't know them.

I remember Lilian who lived a very simply life and said at the age of ninety, 'why do I need two coats, I can only wear one at once'. Jean took it upon herself to take flowers round to the sick and elderly every Sunday after morning service. She did this for over fifty years.

There are those who have been active for such organisations as The National Children's Home and Christian Aid, and organised fund raising for local charities. Whenever there has been a disaster in another part of the world, or in this country, the church has often raised special funds to help alleviate the suffering. All denominations have their own organisations for relief aid work. Believe you me; a huge amount of work is done by churches on behalf of other people.

Z: It seems to me that faith is actually worked out in the nitty gritty of everyday life – not in the secluded cloisters of a monastery or a cathedral. When I am acting the fool and bringing a smile to someone's face it is precisely then that the Kingdom breaks through.

That's right but it doesn't always happen. As you inferred earlier on, there is always a danger that people will use various forms of spiritual techniques simply as a way of furthering their own selfish agenda. Kenneth Leech is a writer who has put this very forcibly, 'much of what is called Christian spirituality today has little to do with Christ or with building up the Christian community. Rather it seeks to promote forms of personal wholeness, inner peace, and enhanced consciousness – all of which may be desirable goals, but they are not what Christian faith is about.' (8) I recently had a knock at my door from two ladies trying to give me some answers about the meaning of life and I asked them what they thought about the war in Iraq. Their reply was, 'it is nothing to do with us'. There you have my point in a nutshell, the danger of people living in a secluded, selfish world, unconcerned about issues of the world. The only concern of the two ladies was with their own spiritual health and well being and anything 'out there' was nothing to do with them. The result is a split spirituality.

Gerard Hughes gives some telling examples of how Christians can have a split spirituality. He argues that this split is apparent in all denominations. 'The charismatics versus the political and social activists, the evangelisers versus the community developers. I know that there are many Christians who both pray and act socially and politically, but they are not the majority and they usually meet with fierce opposition, not from unbelievers, but from their own Christian brothers and sisters.'(9)

Rather than speaking of 'bringing Jesus into my life' as some Christians are prone to do, the New Testament speaks of bringing us into Christ's life. In particular, Paul talks about being in Christ, in Greek, *en Christo*, and he actually uses this phrase one hundred and sixty four times. The implication clearly, is that Christians have to try to live as Christ lived.

Z: Try not to bring Greek into the discussion. Trying to understand things in English is difficult enough. I am much happier talking about love.

The original definition of contemplation did include that word; a long *loving* look at the real. 'Contemplation is not study, not cold examination, not a computer. To contemplate is to be in love.' (10) Another word might be compassion.

Z: I absolutely love chocolate but that is hardly compassion!

That is a different meaning to the word love. C.S. Lewis in his well known book on the subject gives four different meanings to the word love but the meaning that is most often used in the New Testament is that of selfless love. It is not at all easy because it may involve loving our enemies. Just as we saw in the last chapter that prayer can lead to action so this kind of love challenges one's life style. This kind of love means behaving with magnanimity towards other people and being kind to them. Loving is a kind of giving and shows itself in action. This kind of love is about deeds, not words.

Z: Like when you buy your wife a bunch of flowers or take her out for a meal?

That is one way. I think the greatest gift you can give somebody is your time. You show people how much you love them by spending time with them. You also want to communicate with them and listen to them. Remember, Zeno, you listen with your eyes.

Z: That's a new one for me. I thought that's what my ears were for.

The trouble is that loving is not always easy because we live in a society that is very competitive. The more we can attain for ourselves the better it seems. If we have a bigger house, a bigger car, and enjoy ever more exotic holidays then, in the eyes of the world, we have succeeded. The problem is that there is only a certain amount to go round and if one person gets more, then it means that other people get less. It is ironic that about one billion people in the world are starving whilst about one billion are obese. This is contrary to the Christian gospel and the rule of love which is about sharing. One of the biggest selling albums of the last decade was by an American rapper called 50 Cent. Its title speaks for itself, *Get Rich or Die Tryin'*. This is the language of 'must have', the fast car and the fast life.

Z: People lose their health to make money but then lose their money to get their health back.

The ruthless pursuit of money has not been helpful from a national point of view. One has only to look at the appalling mess that bankers have made. The country was brought to the brink of collapse because some people became too greedy.

Z: You could also add the nasty fiasco of MP's expenses. I would certainly get more money kicking a football around, but would I be happy with a television in every room in a top security house, lots of fancy cars and people prying into my every move?

Paul makes a fascinating comment in his letter to the Christians at Philippi. 'I regard everything as loss because of the surpassing value of knowing Christ Jesus my Lord. For his sake I have suffered the loss of all things, and I regard them as rubbish, in order that I may gain Christ.' (Phil. 3: 8)

Z: So it's all rubbish. That's a turn up for the books and certainly a change in priorities.

Well one thing is for sure, we all end up in a box and we can't take our possessions with us. Our last coat does not have any pockets.
'Love is the one "commodity" that is not diminished by sharing. In fact, it is increased. But that takes a lot of believing'. (11)

Z: It reminds me of the children's song:

Love is like a magic penny
Hold it tight and you won't have any
Lend it, spend it
And you'll have so many
They'll all roll over the floor.

In this kind of love, there is certainly no greed, no desire to control, manipulate or dominate. The most perfect example we have of love is the crucifixion and there you can see complete vulnerability in all its nakedness. This is the complete opposite of any form of coercion or manipulation. Notice that love is not the same as like. We are not asked, invited, or indeed commanded, to like everybody.

Z: Thanks goodness for that. A limerick comes to mind.
I do not like thee Dr. Fell.
        The reason why I cannot tell.
But this I know, I know full well.
        I do not like thee Dr. Fell.

That's it exactly. Dr. Fell was a Latin master who was obviously disliked by one of his pupils. We may not know why we don't like somebody – or why we like them. The point is that we look upon them in a loving kind of way. And before you get any ideas, this is not looking upon them with any kind of sexual motive.

Z: I though you might say that but sometimes undesirable thoughts do cross my mind when I look at, say, a pretty young lady.

Perhaps the following prayer will help you.

Teach me your way of looking at people:
as you glanced at Peter after his denial,
as you penetrated the heart of the rich young man
and the hearts of your disciples.

I would like to meet you as you really are
since your image changes those with whom you
come into contact. (12)

Z: That seems to me to be ever so difficult.

Nobody ever said the Christian life is easy. G.K. Chesterton
once said that the Christian life hadn't been given up because
it was too easy, but that it have never been tried because it was
too difficult.

Z: With that sobering thought maybe it is time to move on!

I have tried to show that contemplation can be an escape for
some but that is not the Christian ideal. Moreover, authentic
contemplation actually leads into issues of justice and peace.
Prayer at its best connects us to life. It has been said of Ignatius in
his mature years that he was a contemplative in action. 'What is
seen as incompatible with contemplation is greed, possessiveness,
acquisitiveness, cruelty, indifference to the needs of others,
pride, self-assertiveness, and preoccupation with oneself and
one's public image. But hard work, preoccupation with serving
the needs of others, and so forth, are seen as opportunities to be
contemplative in action.' (13)

Z: Didn't you once tell me that the founder of Methodism,
John Wesley, was an example of someone who put his faith into
action?

I did indeed, but it is only true up to a point because Wesley's main focus was that of personal holiness. However, during his early days at Oxford University he and fellow students formed the 'Holy Club'. Members of this club were very methodical in their lives and they included prayer, studying, attending church services and practising 'good works', including visits to the local, notorious gaol. During his early ministry he had a clinic for the sick in his chapel. In his sermon on the use of money he wrote; 'earn all you can, save all you can and give all you can.' (14) Wesley was determined to die without any savings at all. He received £40,000 from his books but gave it all away. In his last letter Wesley wrote to William Wilberforce urging him to continue his fight against slavery.

Clearly, Wesley was not only concerned with personal holiness but also he had a deep interest in the welfare of others, especially the poor and the prisoner. Moreover, he encouraged his followers to do good to all people not only in spiritual ways but also in practical ways. It was axiomatic for Wesley that people had to do all they could in all the ways they could, as long as they could. Some Methodist preachers were among the original Tolpuddle martyrs and they were in at the beginning of the Trade Union movement. In fact, unions were so strongly influenced by the early Methodists that union lodges were known as chapels and they often began their meetings with prayer. Stephenson, a Methodist minister, provided a house for homeless children in Lambeth in 1869 and so began the National Children's Home.

A more recent example of life in action is the life of Lord Soper, also a Methodist minister. Early in his ministry he pioneered children's Cinema in Islington and every Christmas presided over breakfast for five hundred poor children. From Kingsway Hall in London, he supported those on the margins through various social work schemes. He was also highly concerned with the political issues of the day. One minute he was occupied with relations with Russia, the next with third world poverty, or the welfare state and its problems. He put his weight behind the Campaign for Nuclear Disarmament and the League Against Cruel Sports.

Z: This might surprise you but I actually met Soper a few years before he died. It is important to say that central to his life was the Eucharist. He regarded it as the scaffold upon which everything else was built.

That's right. It is always a case of finding a balance between one's prayer life and one's active engagement with life. If all is functioning well the prayer life leads to the engagement with life and the engagement with life drives us back into prayer. The danger is that of thinking one kind of activity is more spiritual than another. This brings us to the question of what is spirituality.

## Points to Ponder:

1. How do you feel about the idea of going on a retreat?

2. What do you say to someone who says that prayer is an easy way out?

3. Give examples of different kinds of love?

4. What do you think about the statement, 'there can be no spirituality without action?'

5. Give some examples of times where there is nothing you can do except pray.

## Meditation:

'Be still and know that I am God'. Repeat this text from psalm 46 very, very slowly and in the course of time, gradually drop a word off the end until you end up with the one word 'be'.

## References:

1.  Traub, George W., <u>An Ignatian Spirituality Reader</u>, Loyola Press, 2008, p.91
2.  ibid, p.93
3.  de Mello, Anthon, <u>The Song of the Bird</u>, Image, 1984, p.64
4.  Bailey, Simon, <u>The Well Within</u>, DLT, 1996, p.63
5.  ibid.
6.  Leech, Kenneth, <u>Soul Friend,</u> DLT, 1994, p.30
7.  Elliott, Charles, <u>Praying the Kingdom</u>, DLT, 1987, p.146
8.  Leech, Kenneth, <u>The Sky is Red</u>, DLT, 1997, p.122
9.  Hughes, Gerard W., <u>Oh God Why?</u> BRF, 1993, p. 22
10. Traub, op. cit., p.93
11. Jones, Alan, <u>Soul Making</u>, SCM, 1986, p.151
12. Harter, Michael, (ed), <u>Hearts on Fire, Praying with Jesuits</u>, Harter, 2005, p.89
13. Traub, op. cit., p.5
14. Wesley, John, <u>Forty Four Sermons</u>, Epworth, 1946, sermon 44

# Chapter 6

## WHAT IS SPIRITUALITY?

Z: I noticed you have used that word 'spirituality' quite a bit. Would you say I was spiritual?

Certainly. You have the gift of making people laugh and that is a wonderful gift. A well aimed custard pie is an excellent way of deflating a person's self importance. Humour has the ability to be subversive, as with the little boy pointing out that the emperor had no clothes, a person with authority is brought down to size. Pomposity, pretence, and hypocrisy are all punctured. It is no surprise that Hitler placed many comedians, including Charlie Chaplin, on his 'death list'. Hitler did not like to see himself ridiculed.

I know you slip on a banana skin sometimes but that is a way of acknowledging your humanity. People respond to somebody who is truly human and not a fake. 'To be natural is to be holy; but it is very difficult to be natural. To be natural is to be at home with your own nature.' (1) A difficulty is that people often associate the word spiritual with something that is weird or unnatural. That is actually spiritualism and not at all what I am referring to.

For me, personally, spirituality involves the realization there is more to this world than the things we can see. Paul puts this very succinctly, 'we look not at what can be seen but at what cannot be seen, for what can be seen is temporary, but what cannot be seen is eternal'. (2 Cor. 3:18)

Spirituality is about 'how you think about the universe, who you think you are, and what you believe about belief.' (2) To put it more simply, who we are, where we have come from, and what we are about. Using the imagery of John Bunyan and Pilgrim's Progress, where am I on the journey? A spiritual person sees life as a journey whereas the non spiritual person doesn't think there is a journey to make. 'The journey is a more appropriate symbol of the Christian life than a building rooted to the spot.' (3) Other similar words to journey that come to mind are to do with the idea of quest, search or longing. However, to think of life as a linear journey moving from A to B is only half of the problem.

Z: What other kind of journey is there?

It is the journey inwards. 'If there were a spiritual journey, it would be only a quarter-inch long, though many miles deep.' (4) This is entirely in keeping with the desert tradition that we have mentioned before. One of the most well known sayings of the desert fathers is, 'go to your cell and your cell will teach you all you need to know.'

A spiritual person asks the questions, what is life about? Why am I here? A family lives near to me and I see the husband going to work and then the mother takes the two small children to school before going off to work. During school holidays, sometimes Dad stays at home to baby sit, sometimes Mum does and sometimes grandparents are called in to assist. This family could be replicated all over the country. They have a car, a dog, and they take family holidays. What is the purpose of their life? Is it simply to earn money so that they can come home watch television, put the children to bed, have something to eat so they will be fit enough to go to work again in the morning. Is there something more?

Z: I hope you are not by any remote chance passing judgment on that family. Do you remember what it was like for you when you had a young family? Now you are on the lofty ground of retirement you have the time to look back and reflect.

I accept your point entirely. Life was very full and busy to say the least but I was also very fortunate. The fact that I was preaching and leading small groups on the Christian life meant that I jolly well had to find the time to ask some important questions about Life with a capital 'L'. Does life just consist of an endless round of existence? On the face of it, the life of that family is perfectly normal, but what is it all for? To ask questions like that is the beginning of spirituality.

A definition of spirituality I came across that I like is 'what makes us tick'. (5)

Z: That definitely rings a bell for me.

Another aspect of spirituality is not the intricacies of the world and the wonders that have been revealed by scientific endeavour but the fact that the world exists at all.
Why is there anything at all, rather than nothing? Why does it seem there is only life on planet earth? Life is a mystery.

Mother Julian expressed this wonder in the following modern version of her 'shewing'.
God showed me in my palm
a little thing round as a ball
about the size of a hazelnut.
I look at it with the eye of my
understanding and asked myself:
"What is this thing?"

And I was answered: "It is everything that is created."

I wondered how it could survive since
it seemed so little it could suddenly
disintegrate into nothing.

The answer came: "It endures and ever will endure,
because God loves it."

And so everything has being
because of God's love. (6)

In similar fashion William Blake wrote,
To see a World in a grain of sand
And a Heaven in a Wild Flower.
Hold Infinity in the palm of your Hand
And eternity in an hour.... (7)

Z: This is all very well but I wonder whether everybody is spiritual or whether it is just a few.

A quick answer is that everybody is spiritual but they have different ways of expressing their spirituality. For example Benner defines spirituality as 'the response to a deep and mysterious human yearning for self-transcendence and surrender. This yearning results from having been created in such a fashion that we are incomplete when we are self-encapsulated. As important as relationships with other people are, we need something more than involvement with others; something within us yearns for surrender to the service of some person or cause bigger than ourselves. When we experience this self-transcendent surrender, we suddenly realize that we have found our place. It may be that we never before recognized that our restlessness was our search for our place. However, when we find it we immediately know that this is where we belong. Again, spirituality is our response to these longings.' (8)

Z: That was a bit long. I need a bit of time to think about it! I'm not at all sure that everybody is yearning or longing to be involved with something that takes them out of themselves.

Evidence of the fact that we are all spiritual comes from the work of David Hay in Nottingham who has carried out detailed research on that very subject. In one of his early books he quotes an N.O.P. finding that rather more than 36 per cent of their sample had been aware of or influenced by a presence or a power. 'On that basis we could predict that about fifteen million adults in this country would say the same; that is to say, over a third of the population aged sixteen or over.' (9) In more recent unpublished research Hay and Hunt say that the commonest kind of experience reported in Britain is the recognition of a transcendent providence: a patterning of events in a person's life that convinces them that in some strange way those events were meant to happen. Many people felt they have been aware of the presence of God. (10)

This idea of presence is central to spirituality and is something we shall return to in chapter 7. A definition of spirituality is the sense of the divine presence and living in the light of that presence. Many times I have experienced that presence. It goes without saying that we are not in touch with that presence all the time, however hard we might try. As we know only too well, the presence of God can be very elusive.

Z: Just like trying to pin jelly to the ceiling.

Of course, for a Christian the important thing is 'living in the light of that presence'.

Z: That is the hard part.

For many, spirituality is really a matter not of what we experience or think, but how a faith commitment expresses and develops itself in action. For a Christian, life is not only a matter of loving God, but about the outcome of loving God which is to love your neighbour as yourself. To put it another way, Christian spirituality is not just about experiencing God but trying to see things as God does. If God were to look at your church, for example, what would God see? If God were to look at your life, what would God see? St. Paul writes about Christians having the 'mind of Christ'. (1 Cor. 2:16) and Jesus gives a model for mission when he stands up in the synagogue and recites the verses from Isaiah.

He has anointed me to bring good news to the poor.
He has sent me to proclaim release to the captives
and recovery of sight to the blind,
to let the oppressed go free. (Luke 4:18)

Z: I think you wrote all about the need for action as well as prayer in the last chapter so why don't you return to the research. It's good to get some specific data, not just ideas.

Other findings of Hay and Hunt were that people talk of being aware of God when they are very happy. In the latest poll, 38% of the sample said they had personal awareness of such a divine presence. In great unhappiness or fear many people, including those who are uncertain about God's existence, turn to prayer for help. A total of 37% of those recently questioned felt they had received such help. Another commonly reported experience is an awareness of a sacred presence in nature. A total of 29% of the sample felt that they had had this kind of experience. A surprisingly large number of people, 25% of the national sample, felt they had been in touch with someone who had died. More ominously, a quarter of all the people interviewed felt they had been aware of an evil presence.

Z: I'm getting the impression that a lot of people have these so-called spiritual experiences, a third of the population in fact. Do you have to be religious to have these experiences?

Far from it. As Hay and Hunt write 'it seems highly probable that religious awareness is something innate, both because of its universality and its survival value'. (11) Although the particular kind of experience will depend on your religious culture, or lack of it and the way you see things. For example, it is unlikely that a Protestant would have a mystical experience of the Virgin Mary, or, for that matter, of the Buddha. All of us are conditioned by the ideas and events that we have been exposed to and it would be difficult to experience something outside our frame of reference.

Z: So we are not as free as we like to think we are?

That very point of individual freedom comes up in chapter eight. The important question about experience is what we do with the things that we experience. Do we pass from one place to another, taking photographs, but without being touched by the experience?

Z: Like the apocryphal America tourist who 'does' Europe in five days but doesn't 'see' anything.

Exactly. In a sense it is a question of whether I am a tourist or a pilgrim. *'Spirituality is and is not a matter of experience. It is not mainly about experiences so much as experience.'* (12). The latter is the way we have interpreted the former and what difference they have made to our lives. Have our experiences simply been events during the course of our lives or have they had an emotional effect to such an extent that we have been changed by them. For example, it could be said that I had experiences whilst on a thirty day silent retreat. The important thing is not the day by day events as such but how the whole retreat changed me. Thus we speak about an 'experienced' person and this is not just to say they have been on lots of different holidays or worked in different places. It is to say that the person has taken on board those experiences and become a different person. Spirituality is being aware – tuned in to what God may be saying to us at any moment.

Z: You are repeating yourself my friend. You mentioned the importance of being aware in chapter four.

Yes, I know. The chapter headings are somewhat artificial because there is so much overlap between the subjects I am discussing. David Hay writes that spiritual awareness is a necessary part of our human make-up, biologically built into us, whatever our religious beliefs or lack of them. Spiritual awareness is a human universal; it is 'hard-wired' into the human organism. Hence, it cannot be limited to members of any particular religion or indeed religious people in general. Everybody, including people who hold no religious beliefs whatsoever, is created with the potential to be a spiritual being.

Z: I am just about hanging in there. My struggle is that I have always associated being spiritual with being religious.

That is not the case. The problem is there are all sorts of negative connotations associated with religion. Religion is perceived to be rigid and hierarchical whereas spirituality is perceived to be much more open, egalitarian and creative. Spirituality tends to avoid definitions. Religion is equated with the church that often appears to be old fashioned, moralistic, out of touch, authoritarian and boring. Religion is about the formal and institutional structure of belief; Judaism, Hinduism, Islam, Christianity, and others belong to this category. Some would even go so far as to say that religion is life denying but spirituality is life affirming. Others go further and say they are a believer but they are definitely not religious.

Z: They don't go to church – unless they are carried in!

In other words, being spiritual is not the same as being religious, furthermore spirituality is not necessarily Christian; all religions have their spiritualities. One could even say there are different kinds of Christian Spirituality. Roman Catholic spirituality has tended to concentrate on things like liturgy, confession, religious rites such as the sacraments, making a retreat and the need for spiritual guidance usually from a priest. On the other hand Protestant Spirituality has been more individualistic, concentrating on the direct line between the believer and God without the need for a priest as a go between. The latter has also focussed more on the Word of God as found in scripture and as preached, as opposed to rites and liturgy. Faber interestingly points out that in Roman Catholic worship the medium of God's revelation is the eye, whereas in Protestant worship the medium of God's revelation is the ear. (13). This difference in emphasis is often highlighted by church architecture, although, in recent years, the polarity is not so marked. The types of spirituality are no longer mutually exclusive and this can be seen in the changing architecture of modern church buildings. For example, at the turn of the last century a typical non conformist church would have been dominated by a central pulpit and the communion table would have been almost insignificant by comparison. Today, this would not be the case.

Z: Talking of church buildings I wonder what Peter or Paul would think if they were alive today and saw the great huge cathedrals built in their names?

I wonder too, but let's not get sidetracked. Spirituality is not always 'good'. Adolph Hitler was a spiritual being, a man 'possessed', more than most, yet his spirit was surely evil. The New Testament encourages us to test the spirits to see if they are of God. 'Beloved, do not believe every spirit, but test the spirits to see whether they are of God'. (1 John 4:1) One way of 'testing the spirits' is to consider your feelings.

Z: That is easier said than done.

I know that only too well. I was in my early thirties before I went on a counselling course and the first question we were asked was 'what are you feeling?' I had no idea! We can have lots of feelings but I want to suggest for the moment that there are 'worldly feelings' and 'otherworldly feelings'. Imagine you are being appreciated, applauded, praised; you get to the top, you are successful, you win the race or argument and there is a sense of elation. That is a worldly feeling. Think about the times when you have power, everyone is looking up to you. That is a worldly feeling. These experiences are not lasting and they don't lead to happiness, only to excitement, emptiness, and anxiety. What are other people thinking or saying about me?

Z: Yes, but don't forget that what other people think about you is none of your business.

That is very helpful Zeno. Contrast these feelings with looking at a sunset, walking through freshly fallen snow or autumn leaves, gazing up at the night sky or watching the ebb and flow of the tide; or doing some work that you love – a hobby, watching a good film or reading a good book or being in the company of some good friends. In all these examples you are more aware and more awake. That is being spiritual. It is energizing and brings you to life.

A friend of mine is a garden designer. She used to go to church regularly but now only attends on high days and holidays. Her undoubted spirituality finds fulfillment in the natural world. For example, she will have moments of ecstatic enjoyment when she discovers a rare orchid. Another friend would not describe herself as at all religious and would hesitate to mention God in conversation. Nevertheless she regularly goes on a retreat to find space and peace. Whilst there, she usually does nothing except embroider. At home, her times of quiet and reflection take place as she embroiders. Other friends go for long walks, or engage in gardening or wood carving.

Z: That is more like my kind of spirituality.

## Images of God

For Christians their spirituality is derived from their particular notion of God

Z: Do you mean like an old man in the sky with a long beard and rather stern face?

That is a very anthropomorphic way of looking at God.

Z: Anthro what?

Sorry. I said there wouldn't be any long words. It simply means attributing human characteristics and behaviour to God. To say that God is stern, has a beard or indeed, has a face, is being anthropomorphic. For obvious reasons God is not in the sky either so when people recite the Nicene Creed which contains the phrase 'he ascended into heaven' there is a danger of great confusion.

Z: I'm told that in Norwich cathedral there is a medieval depiction of Jesus' ascension showing his hemline and the soles of his feet disappearing into the clouds.
I'm trying to think of a suitable footnote!

All I can say is that religious metaphors need a lot of unpacking. As with many other aspects of our personality and spirituality our early experiences provide us with our own particular model of God. I once preached on the fatherhood of God and received a vitriolic letter from a lady the following day saying that she could not see that God was a father because she had received such ghastly treatment from her own earthly father. The image of God as father was anathema to her. Gerard Hughes gives the example of dear Uncle George. (14) He is a very frightening figure who deals savagely with those who are not well behaved. Children are encouraged to love this great uncle who is nothing other than an ogre. Of course, adults don't generally perceive God as an ogre but, nevertheless, they may have the same feelings of fear, if not absolute terror, if they think they are in God's presence.

Z: Can you give another less dramatic example?

There is a modern religious song that has the words:
> Till on that cross as Jesus died,
> The wrath of God is satisfied –

What kind of image of God does that present? I find the thought of God getting angry and so crucifying his son totally abhorrent and completely contrary to any ideas one might entertain about God being a God of love. Indeed that is the biblical definition of God par excellence: God is love. God may well get angry but it is not a loving thing to do to crucify anyone let alone a person with whom you have such a special relationship.

Z: That's still quite a dramatic example.

In a book called Mister God this is Anna, Fynn the author puts these words into the mouth of Anna. 'In whatever way or state you understand Mister God, so you diminish his size. He becomes an understandable entity among other understandable entities. So Mister God keeps on shedding bits all the way through your life until the time comes when you admit freely and honestly that you don't understand

Mister God at all. At this point you have let Mister God be his proper size and wham; there he is laughing at you.' (15)

Z: I like the idea of God laughing. If I were the finger of God and all the world were ticklish..........

I must say it is a thought that has not been in traditional theology at all.

Z: Do you mean the idea of God tickling?

Very funny Zeno

Z: Anyway I think you used the word theology\*\*!!\*\*??!! What do you mean?

Theology is just a short hand way of saying what people are doing when they talk about God. In traditional theology God has been defined as all powerful (omnipotent), all present (omnipresent) and knowing all things (omniscient). We now live in a world where these concepts are challenged if not explicitly then certainly implicitly. If God is all powerful then why is there so much suffering and pain in the world? Why are so many people hungry and thirsty?

Z: I read something the other day which made me think. 'The puzzle is not why God allows the poor to starve. The scandal is why God allows the rich not to share'. (16)

That certainly puts the boot on the other foot! However, as we saw in chapter two the feeding of the 5000 can be interpreted as a parable about sharing. The question though, for some people, remains the same. Why doesn't God do something about it? That is precisely the question that was asked hundreds of years ago by Job when he was afflicted by pain and suffering. This is not the place to write about the problem of suffering. Erudite tomes have been written on precisely that subject. Suffice it to say that the problem only becomes a problem when God is pictured as totally omnipotent, that is, all-controlling, entirely responsible for anything and everything. This is the God who wonderfully waves a magic wand when things go wrong and abracadabra everything is put right again.

A few days ago I parked in a supermarket car park and went in to do some shopping completely forgetting to buy a parking ticket. I returned to find a fine had been placed on my windscreen. I was more than a little annoyed and irritated but God probably just smiled and said 'you silly Billy'.

Z: Are you being anthro something or other?!

Probably, but one thing is for sure. God did not step in to pay the fine. Nor did a cheque for £30 mysteriously appear through my letter box. Perhaps I should have prayed about it. Do I want to believe in this kind of God who is there to protect me from my own stupidity or who steps into human affairs at the drop of a hat? If people thought that anything they did wrong would immediately be corrected then I think that would not only make people more irresponsible, it would also make the world very unpredictable. If a child puts his hand into a flame and the flame suddenly loses its capacity to burn, life would be very difficult to deal with. The laws of science would have no meaning. Somebody once remarked that God keeps all the rules especially the rule of love. More of that shortly but, for the moment, let us return to some theology.

Z: I was afraid of that.

Classical theology attributes to God the metaphysical attributes and describes God as infinite, omnipotent, omniscient, omnipresent and the like. The method is simple. One takes a pair of ultimate opposites and one decides in each case which member of the pair is good or admirable and then attributes it to God but not attributing the contrasting term. Classical theology, therefore, describes God as strong rather than weak, eternal not temporal, acting not acted upon, cause not effect, necessary but not contingent and so on. The method takes one pole of the contrasting pair for, the theory states; God alone illustrates the superior pole, free from any mixture from the contrasting pole. God is 'the absolute'. I find this kind of God a very abstract kind of notion and one to whom I find it difficult to relate to.

A different kind of theology was developed in the early part of the twentieth century by the Anglo-American philosopher Alfred North Whitehead. This is called process theology and it has become increasingly influential and further developed by Hartshorne in the United States. Process theology affirms both poles of each pair of ultimate opposites in order to characterise God. Both aspects are in their most supreme form. However, as soon as we admit that each category and also its contrary have a supreme form then either we have the idea of two supreme beings or we have the idea of one supreme being with two really distinct aspects – to one of which the supreme case of a category applies, such as, strength and to the other its contrasting category applies, that is, weakness. Process theology thus affirms a kind of bipolar view of God rather than two supreme beings. Let us take the example of omnipotence in order to clarify the issue.

Z: Some clarity would be most welcome!

As we have seen, to claim that God is omnipotent raises all sorts of questions. We therefore have to ask the question whether God is, or has, unlimited power. Process theologians would argue that God has the power to accomplish that which he wants to, rather than say he can do anything whatsoever.

A similar argument arises when we apply the notion of God as Infinite. God is indeed 'infinite' beyond any such limitation as our minds might devise, but this does not mean he is <u>absolutely</u> unlimited. His nature, the purpose which he is accomplishing in the world, the love which is his supreme characteristic, must in some sense, limit him.

It is significant that the nearest the bible gets to a definition of God is, 'God is love' (I John 4:8). 'What if God's love and not his power shapes the way he relates to his world?' (17) Love by its very nature does not constrain. It always gives freedom and space to the beloved. A parent gives space to their child to crawl, to toddle, to fall over, to explore, to bump themselves, to hurt themselves. The alternative is to lock the child away in a padded cot within a padded room. Such a cotton wool existence would not be a loving thing to do. In the same way God gives us our freedom. The ancient story about the Garden of Eden is the story of Adam being given the freedom, to do what he is forbidden from doing, to eat the fruit from the tree of the knowledge of good and evil. God is willing to live with the consequences.

Anthony de Mello tells a parable for religious educators. It is the story of a sheep who finds a hole in a fence. The sheep wandered far and was lost but the shepherd eventually found it and brought it back. In spite of everyone urging him to the contrary, the shepherd refused to nail up the hole in the fence. (18)

Z: I wonder whether he lost many of his sheep.

The ultimate symbol of love, the cross, is not about power or coercion. Quite the opposite. God demonstrates through Jesus his weakness and vulnerability. Herein is the creative power of the cross. To that extent God is powerless.

Therefore He Who Thee reveals
Hangs, O Father, on that Tree
Helpless; and the nails and thorns
Tell of what Thy love must be. (19)

As Bonhoeffer writes, ' God is weak and powerless in the world, and that is exactly the way, the only way, in which he can be with us and help us.......only a suffering God can help.' (20) It is precisely this which gives us hope because it demonstrates that God is with us in our pain and suffering, not remote or abstract. The Christian belief is that God became human and literally put himself into human hands.

Z: The thought of God being in my hands makes me feel very responsible – quite a new feeling for me.

Another example from classical theology is the notion of God as perfect. God is defined as 'that than which nothing greater can be conceived', that is, the greatest conceivable concept of an absolutely perfect being. As a result of this definition God's perfection is regarded as a wholly static state, an absolute which cannot be changed. Hartshorne rejects this view. He argues that God is always unsurpassable by others, but at the same time he is surpassable by himself. In other words the content of his knowledge at time T2 will surpass the content of his knowledge at time T1 if things have happened between T1 and T2. As perfect, he will know all there is to know at time T1 without loss or error and at T2 all that is knowable without loss or error. There can be no ultimate totality of actualities for anyone to know and therefore God, in order to be omniscient, must admit change. To this extent the process doctrine is of a God who is totally involved in the cosmic process and in time, so much so that God moves along with them. God is therefore only omniscient of the past and present, not the future. For me this is encouraging because it leaves open the future; everything is not absolutely predetermined. If everything in the future is already decided I have no free will at all.

Z: I think it's time you left this theology and got back to something I can understand.

It seems to me that some people are hanging on to the church by the tips of their fingers. Why is this? A possibly reason is that they can no longer go along with the type of theology, classical theology, which comes through a lot of hymns, liturgy and preaching.

Z: You are in danger of overstating your case. Some churches are clearly full, some churches in other parts of the world are growing very quickly, and some people are very satisfied with their church.

I know there is always another view point but an interesting comment comes from an unexpected source. Rob Frost, was a well known evangelist, who died a few years ago, and he wrote, 'I am deeply disillusioned with what the church is offering Sunday by Sunday. There is a deadness in the ritual, a dryness in the formality, and a growing irrelevance in the institution. At least I find a genuine hunger for spiritual things in the New Age community, an openness to try new ideas, and a deep respect for the beliefs of others'. (21). Note that this is Rob Frost, who was well known for his evangelical views, finding succour for his spiritual journey in very unexpected places. He says though, that he has not lost his 'evangelical marbles.' (22) Somebody else once said that modern church services have about as much feeling for the numinous as the average bus station. John Drane reckons that the church is in danger of becoming a secular institution in a spiritual age. (23)

Z: But I thought that some churches were growing.

My guess is that churches that are growing have taken on board some of the post modern assumptions that I mentioned in chapter seven. There is fragmentation, no longer does one size liturgy fit all, and so there is a desire to write new liturgies which are more appropriate to a particular context. The same is true for hymns. Many people, especially the young, are not satisfied with the old classic hymns. So long as they are appropriate, songs are taken from a variety of sources and so diversity has become the norm. There is also a hunger in growing churches, a search for meaning.
Finally, there is a 'hanging loose' from the institution.

Z: You may well be right but I had the feeling that these churches are often more theologically conservative.

That is true in the main but research shows that although these churches have a big front door they also have a very large back door. People tend to outgrow them.
Jamieson has written about this in 'A churchless faith'. (24)

My feeling is that people are looking for more relevant ways of expressing their faith. The old classic notions explicit or implicit in our liturgies have run their course. If we took on board some of the findings of process theology I think there would be more openness, flexibility, and diversity. There would be less desire to have everything, including God, all wrapped up and more of a wish to search for truth and involve others in that search. 'It is now clearly on the Church's agenda that.....worship must be open, honest, flexible, and responsive with respect to the prevailing culture.' (25)

Richter and Francis talk about 'authentic worship' and quote the theologian Martyn Percy, 'the key concern ... is a style of worship which does not offer any real theological basis for individuals to mature in their faith. The danger is that once people have become bored with anodyne and escapist worship they will not move on to a style which allows room for spiritual development. They will simply chuck the whole product away.' (26)

Z: So we've come back to spirituality but I would really like you to tackle the big questions. Is there a God at all?

I can but try.

## Points to ponder:

1. How would you define spirituality?

2. Are you a religious person or a spiritual person or a mixture of both?

3. What is God like for you?

4. Where do you see your church in, say, ten years time?

5. What ideas about God come through a typical church service?

## Meditation:

Imagine God is looking at you right now. What does God see?

Imagine God is looking at your church. What does God see?

## References

1.  O'Donohue, John, <u>Anam Cara</u>, Bantam books, 1999, p.133
2.  Drane, John. <u>Do Christians know how to be Spiritual?</u>, DLT, 2005, p.25
3.  Holloway, Richard, <u>Dancing on the Edge</u>, Fount, 1997, p. 159
4.  O'Donohue, op. cit., p.120
5.  Wakefield, Gordon. S, <u>Groundwork of Christian Spirituality</u>, Epworth, 2001, p. 1
6.  Doyle Brendan, <u>Meditations with Julian of Norwich</u>, Bear and Company, 1986 p.25
7.  Blake, William, <u>Auguries of Innocence,</u> Grossman publishers, 1968, p.431-2
8.  Benner, David, <u>Psychotherapy and the Spiritual Quest</u>, Hodder & Stoughton , 1989, p.104
9.  Hay, David, <u>Exploring Inner Space</u> , Pelican 1982, p.118
10. Understanding the spirituality of people who

don't go to church. A report on the findings of the Adults' Spirituality Project at the University of Nottingham, David Hay & Kate Hunt 2000

11. ibid. p.195

12. Thompson Ross, Christian Spirituality , SCM, 2008, p.122

13. Faber, Heije, Above the Treeline, SCM, 1988, p.19

14. Hughes, Gerard W., God of Surprises, DLT, 1983, p.34

15. Fynn, Mister God, this is Anna, Collins, 1980, p. 118

16. Runcorn, David, Choice, desire and The Will Of God, SPCK, 2003, p.68

17. ibid., p.13

18. de Mello, Anthony, The Song of the Bird, Image Books, 1982, p156

19. Vanstone W.H, Love's Endeavour, Love's Expense, DLT, 1979, p119

20. Bonhoeffer, Dietrich, Letters & Pateps From Prison, Fontana, 1965, p. 122

21. Frost , Rob, New Age Spirituality, Kingsway Publications, 2001, p. 9

22. ibid. p.10

23. Drane, John, The McDonaldization of the Church, DLT, 2000, p.54

24. Jamieson, Alan, A Churchless Faith, SPCK, 2003

25. Saxbee, John, Liberal Evangelism, SPCK, 1994, p.70

26. Richter, Philip, and Francis, Leslie, J. Gone but not forgotten, DLT, 1998, p.108

# Chapter 7

## WHATEVER HAPPENED TO GOD?

Present day writers on spirituality seem to take it as read that God exists but they make no effort to say who or what God is for them. To state the obvious since we cannot see God it is difficult to say what God is like or, indeed, that God exists. The New Testament asserts that God is invisible (John 1:18, 6:46, I Tim. 6:16, I John 4:12) and, indeed, if God were visible then he/she could hardly be called God.

Z: There are lots of things you can't see but you know they are there. The wind is an obvious example and I don't mean the kind of wind that you often have. Don't forget also the oxygen we breathe in every moment of our lives. If that disappeared we would soon know about it. On second thoughts, we wouldn't be alive to tell anyone.

Good examples. God has also been likened to a force like gravity. The problem is that personal attributes have been ascribed to God in a way that could not be ascribed to gravity. Gravity could not be described as loving. It is an impersonal force with no human characteristics whatsoever. It is one thing to argue that traditional concepts of God have long since become dated and irrelevant, but how, then, do we describe

God? Robinson in his theological best seller described God as 'the ultimate depth of all our being, the creative ground and meaning of all our existence'. (1)

Z: I like the sound of that but what on earth does it mean?

For Robinson, God is what matters most in our lives, 'what you take seriously without any reservation.' (2) This is not a question of whether '*a* Being exists beyond the bright blue sky, or anywhere else.' (3) Belief is what you take seriously without any reservation.

Z: Dare I say that I think he is wrong. It matters a great deal whether God exists or not or whether God is an illusion.

I suppose it all depends what you mean by existence. For a mathematician the square root of minus one exists. It is denoted by the letter 'i'

Z: Now I really am lost.

The square root of minus one is simply a concept, a working hypothesis that allows mathematicians to find the square root of negative numbers as well as positive numbers.

Z: I never could do arithmetic anyway. Incidentally, why are the Chinese good at arithmetic? Because they can do take-aways.

Very funny. Let's get back to the point. It could be argued that God is a concept, a working hypothesis. Certainly, for me personally, the idea of God allows me to make sense of the world. God is a reality that defies description and all our words are inadequate. Some would argue that to suggest that God exists is to apply a human characteristic to God.

Z: You are beginning to lose me again.

Sorry. The difficulty is that many claim we have simply attributed to God human characteristics. The German theologian, Feuerbach, was one of the major contributors to this debate. He argued that God is a projection of 'man', God is made in the image of 'man'. All theology is thus reduced to anthropology, a study of the human species. This was an argument later adopted by Freud.

Z: Can this argument be refuted?

Well there is some truth in it. Especially in the early days of the bible, not to mention the Greek and Roman gods of ancient mythology, God was attributed with human characteristics. In Genesis we read that God was 'walking in the garden at the time of the evening breeze.' (Gen. 3: 8) It is all too easy to project human traits on to God.

The difficulty is that of trying to describe God at all. For example, Robinson in a book called 'Exploration into God' says, 'from one point of view, the meaningless monosyllable 'God' simply stands for an 'x'....signifying that which cannot be expressed yet cannot be eliminated.' (4)

Z: The x factor. Sounds like a television programme.

It is simply a way of saying that to a large extent we know very little about God. There is nothing new in this. In the Old Testament the prophet Isaiah wrote 'for my thoughts are not your thoughts, nor are your ways my ways, says the

Lord.' (Is.55:8) Many have asserted that there is 'an infinite qualitative difference' between God and people. I have always been uncomfortable with those who think they know all there is to know about God. They have God all wrapped up in their back pocket.

Z: But aren't you forgetting that Jesus points us in the direction of God?

You are thinking of the texts in John's gospel. 'No one has ever seen God. It is God the only Son, who is close to the Father's heart, who has made him known.' (1:18) a few chapters later Jesus says to Philip, 'Whoever has seen me has seen the Father.' (14:9) Obviously Jesus gives us many insights into the nature of God. However, God is not identical to Jesus any more than my sons are identical to me.

Z: I think they would be very glad to hear that.

They carry some of my characteristics, not to mention my genes, but my sons are not me. We have gone someway along the road of saying what God is like but the trouble is that in trying to explain God we can only use words and in the end words are very inadequate. They are simply pointers.

Z: I suppose the important thing is not to look at the pointers but to what is being pointed to. The sign post only gives the direction; it is not the actual destination.
But what does the word 'God' point to? When people use the word it must refer to something.

Traditionally, as we have seen in the last chapter, God was the superior being, the all knowing, the ever present, the all powerful One, 'God is *over everything*, and thus he is *above us*, he is *absolutely superior* to us. That is the only way in which he can be considered.'(5) This is the God who intervenes, apparently at a moment's notice, who heals, who works miracles, who transcends all natural laws, for whom nothing is impossible.

Z: I think you are going to say that many people no longer believe this.

Some certainly do. Let's be honest. There are those who have seen what they believe to be a dramatic action of God in their lives. They have seen a dramatic healing which, they say, can only be accounted for by the action of God. However, for many others, their experience is quite different. The two world wars of the last century were a major turning point in how people thought about God. In one sense the twentieth century began in August 1914 with the outbreak of World War I. This decisive event meant that theology could no longer go on speaking about God in the same way that it had done in the past. Indeed, the question arose as to whether it was possible at all for theologians to speak of God.

Z: No doubt some did.

For sure they did. Karl Barth, for one, was anxious to return to the classical faith of the Reformers, a faith, which he maintained, was based unconditionally on God's revelation and not on any human reason. God is revealed in three ways, the incarnate Word, that is Jesus, the Word of scripture and the Word of proclamation.

In his early writings Barth gives the now famous imagery of the 'wholly other' breaking in upon 'man', 'perpendicularly from above.' This is a theology of revelation, a revelation which breaks in upon the world, a return to classical theology.

However, the insights of liberal theology have taken root, in particular, the conviction that any belief is open to question. It is often said that once people go to university to study theology they become very liberal in their outlook.

Z: Ah yes, killing Christianity by degrees.

If Christianity is not open to questioning and criticism I very much fear for its future. The whole point of education is surely to enable people to deal with questions in a critical kind of way and not with preconceived judgements. Protestantism grew out of the cradle of criticism.

There are those who would argue that openness to secular culture which was a characteristic of Liberal Protestantism continues today with a far greater force and that the theology of the Barthian era was simply a theology of crisis, In other words, it was an interruption rather than a complete reversal of the secularising trend.

Z: What effects did World War II have?

It is interesting to note that the far greater horrors of the second world war did not produce a similar reaction to those of the first world war. The questions now raised tended to be anthropological rather than theological in character: 'how could people do this?' rather than 'how could God allow this?' In other words there was a reticence in applying traditional views of God in an attempt to discover the meaning of the horrific events. A notable exception was Ulrich Simon's 'A theology of Auschwitz.' (6) Simon poses among other questions, how does Auschwitz stand in the light of the Fatherhood of God? In the main, however, the authenticity and relevance of the Christian faith, as stated in orthodox terms was seriously questioned. As Zahrnt put it in the introduction to his book, 'the Christian proclamation, in its traditional form at least, no longer provides the majority of men today with a valid answer to the questions they ask about God, and consequently fails to provide them with an adequate way of understanding their position in the world and of mastering their lives meaningfully.' (7) Bonhoeffer wrote, 'how is it that this war, unlike any of those before it, is not calling forth any "religious" reaction?' (8)

Z: Does that mean that a lot of people are atheists?

That all depends what you mean by atheism. Nearly fifty hears ago Robinson wrote a book in which was a chapter entitled 'Can a truly contemporary person *not* be an atheist?' (9)

Z: I thought he was a bishop in the Church of England.

Yes, he was. A few years earlier a famous Methodist preacher called Leslie Weatherhead wrote a book called 'The Christian Agnostic,' believing that stance to be the only legitimate one that a Christian could make. (10) The title resonates well for those who dislike answers being dictated to them. Some truths are discovered out of the crucible of experience not shouted from pulpits.

Z: Two metres above contradiction.

To return to Robinson, he describes three different kinds of atheism. Firstly, God is intellectually superfluous. This is where people seem to have no need of 'the God hypothesis.' God is not needed to explain the physical world because that is the proper domain of science. The idea of a supernatural being affecting their everyday lives is just not an issue. It is unnecessary.

Z: I guess it is not an issue for you either.

We shall see in the next chapter on freedom that we have been given freedom and if God constantly intervened that would take away our freedom. God is not going to do for us what we are not prepared to do for ourselves. Not only that, if God does intervene then the interventions seem to be completely at random. People can develop cancer or be killed in a car crash regardless of whether they say their prayers or not. The majority of people, at least those in the under forty age bracket get on with their lives without referring to God and certainly the notion of going to church is simply not on their agenda. They eat, sleep, go to work, and have fun, quite literally without the God hypothesis.

Z: Except in times of crisis when they probably say a quick prayer.

That is true, but that brings me to the second kind of atheism where God is emotionally dispensable. People are no longer leaning on God as a kind of emotional crutch, they are learning to be responsible for their own lives. They are aware of the Freudian criticism of religion that it is a universal neurosis and the Marxist criticism that it is the 'opium of the people'.

Z: Has religion been a drug or a crutch for you?

God in Jesus is not a crutch for me, more of an inspiration. Furthermore, God never says that he will take away our sufferings or pain, but he promises to be with us in it. As Paul says, 'nothing in all creation can separate us from the love of Christ.' (Roms.8:38-39) As for being a drug, you only need to read the Sermon on the Mount to realise how difficult it is to be a Christian and if taken at face value it certainly does not have a soporific effect. Quite the reverse.

Z: What about the third kind of atheism?

This is where God is morally intolerable. In other words 'a God who 'causes' or 'allows' the suffering of a single child is morally intolerable.' (11) How can there be a God when there are so many tragedies in the world? There is a real force to this kind of atheism. However, I am sure that God doesn't want people to suffer either. How can any parent want any of their family to suffer? This is precisely the problem that is grappled with in a recent best selling novel. (12) I am reminded of a cartoon I once saw in which somebody said 'sometimes I think I would like to ask God why he allows poverty, famine, and injustice when he could do something about it'. Another person asks, 'What's stopping you?' to which the first person replies, 'I'm afraid he might ask me the same question.'

Z: Let me get this right. If God is intellectually superfluous, is emotionally dispensable and is morally intolerable, where does that leave us? Can anyone call themselves a Christian?

Many people seek refuge in the historical figure of Jesus. Their faith becomes grounded in him. It is not just the life of Jesus that rings bells but the suffering Jesus. As we saw in the last chapter Bonhoeffer explicitly states, 'it is not some religious act which makes a Christian what he is, but participation in the suffering of God in the life of the world.' (13) In the seventies Moltmann wrote a seminal book entitled

'The Crucified God' (14) and a little later Jüngel explicitly stated 'for responsible Christian usage of the word "God," the Crucified One is virtually the real definition of what is meant with the word "God." Christian theology is therefore fundamentally the theology of the Crucified One.' (15)

In a sense there is nothing new in this. The New Testament asserts that God is known through the Son. It is only the Son who knows the Father and hence it is only through the Son that one can know the Father. (Matt. 11:27, John 1:18, 6:46) The implication is that just as Jesus suffers so does God. Any parent suffers when they see their child in pain.

Z: But can you say what God is like for you?

I can only say what God is like for me. Other people have their own views. God is nearer to me than my own breathing, nearer to me than I am to myself. God is the one who is revealed in each moment of time, if only I had the awareness to acknowledge this. Occasionally, in moments of great clarity I experience God. This can be during times of silence, during a communion service, walking by the sea, or whilst washing up the dishes. Notice that these occasions do not happen very often.

Z: You mean you don't wash the dishes very often.

Very funny. There is an elusive quality about God. As already noted, supremely God is known in the life of the suffering Jesus who gives a pattern of life for us. It is a life of perfect love of which we all fall short but, thankfully, God forgives us because the love on offer is completely unconditional and, moreover, it is a love from which we cannot be separated.

Even with the help of the Holy Spirit, most of the time, we all fall short of living the life of love. No one is perfect.

Z: Welcome to the human race!

In my previous book I have written at length about my experiences of God on a thirty day silent retreat. (16) I'm not sure whether to call my experiences the result of interacting with a being or an entity or a force, but it was certainly with something that I am prepared to call God. For me, God is 'something' that can be encountered and that 'something' is also personal because it is an encounter of love.

God is the One who can be encountered in a variety of ways and, more than that, who gives a vision for life. Wouldn't this world be completely different if more people sought the power of love instead of the love of power, if more people took their snouts out of the trough and were more prepared to share, if people genuinely loved themselves and their neighbour, if there was a real desire to seek genuine happiness instead of cheap thrills?

Z: Steady on old boy, when you get on that high horse of yours you are completely beyond my reach.

Thanks for bringing me down to earth I was getting carried away but that is what happened to the first Christians. They were accused of 'turning the world upside down.'(Acts 17:6) There is something utterly compelling about the life of Jesus. I wonder what it was about him that made grown men and women give up their daily jobs, leave everything, and follow him.

In one sense, it is easy to talk about Jesus. The fact that he lived, and died a horrible death, are indisputable historical facts. It is much harder to pin down God. The word God, after all, is only a pointer to something beyond, which is ultimately a mystery but which, for me, is real. God has been defined as 'the mystery that lets us be,' (17) and the title of Jüngel's book gives the game away, 'God as the Mystery of the World.' (18 )

Z: Do we send for Sherlock Holmes to solve the mystery?

No. It is not a mystery in the sense of a whodunit, a mystery that can be solved, but a mystery in the sense of being beyond description and beyond understanding. The anonymous fourteenth century mystic got it about right when he said that God can not be known by our thinking. God is beyond reason and knowledge. '...of God himself can no man think. .....he may well be loved, but not thought. By love he can be caught and held, but by thinking never.' (19)

Z: This is all very well but some may say you are hiding behind this mystery. You are deluding yourself.

They might, but I can only answer that this mystery has had a profound effect on my life. Not only has it provided direction, inspiration and energy, there has been great consolation when I have gone through difficult times and there has been a sense of inner peace, wholeness and inner freedom. If you want objective data, just look at the rise of the early church. Would the first Christians have been prepared to face death and martyrdom if they thought they were deluded? The story of the rise of the early church in the Acts of the Apostles is fascinating. In the midst of the Roman Empire, with the ever present threat of persecution, Christians were prepared to stand up and be counted, even if it meant death. Today, many people in the West take the presence of Christianity for granted. Their attitude is one of supreme indifference. The fact that lives have been changed or that so many noteworthy things have been done by Christians throughout the ages, matters little.

Z: I have to say I'm not yet convinced. Although you have provided some objective data as you say, your evidence seems to be all down to your experience. That seems very subjective to me.

I agree but we can't deny our experience. It is the stuff of life. The question is how we interpret our experience. There are all sorts of dimensions to an experience, sociological, psychological, biological, physiological and so on. For example, we can experience things quite differently if we are with other people, or very tired, or stressed, or in love, or hungry.

Z: I thought food might come into it somewhere.

I would argue that there is also a spiritual dimension to life. William Barry talks about this at length in one of his books about spiritual direction. He suggests that all of life is an encounter. 'There is no human experience that is not encounter.......even the most 'subjective' experience for example, an hallucination, happens to a person who is encountering the air, the ground, the forces of gravity, etc. of the universe, and these 'objective' elements impinge on and condition the experience.' (20)

Developing the work of the Scottish philosopher Macmurray and the American philosopher Smith, Barry maintains that we encounter God through the universe that God has created. In the same way, if you are reading this book that

I have created you encounter me. I am very much part of the book, indeed, in a very real way, I am in every word. Of course, I am also separate from the book and am certainly not identical to it.

Z: That's pretty obvious.

So, if I could use just a little bit of jargon, in the same way God is immanent in the world but also transcendent to it.

Z: Please don't use any more jargon.

O.K. All of this begs the question as to whether it is actually God who I encounter in my experience. Any experience can be interpreted quite differently. If I listen to Beethoven's fifth symphony, although the notes played are exactly the same, what I hear will be quite different to what the conductor hears, or the first violinist, or my wife or anybody else.

Z: Including Beethoven!

In the end to interpret something in a spiritual way comes down to faith. 'The religious dimension of human experience is supplied by the believing and seeking person *and* by the Mystery encountered.' (21)

Z: So it is a question of faith, believing that there is a Mystery to be encountered.

Indeed. As Barry says, 'faith and experience mutually reinforce one another.' (22)

I would find it very difficult to explain, or rationalise, some of my experiences on retreat, or in my life generally, if I didn't believe in God. The experience then reinforces my belief in God. Some would argue that all experiences can have a religious dimension although, to be honest, one might be hard pressed at times to find it. 'Whether we know it or not, God is ingredient in every human experience.' (23) Certainly we are not always on the look out for God. We are too preoccupied with other things.

Z: Just too busy I guess. If you don't stop to admire the daisies you'll soon be pushing them up.

Thanks for that cheerful comment. Another thing to note is that there is a difference between a generally acceptable proposition, for example, Jesus was born in Bethlehem, and an interpretation that we put on that event, for example, Jesus was sent from heaven by God. Difficulties arise when we mix up the two approaches. Was Jesus born of a virgin? Is that a historical event or an interpretation that we put on the birth of Jesus? Only one gospel alludes to the virgin birth and St. Paul has nothing to say on the matter. Indeed, he doesn't mention the birth of Jesus, nor does Mark, the first gospel writer. To suggest something is historical when it is not is to put Christians in the position of having to believe a few impossible things before breakfast everyday.

Z: Perhaps they need to stop eating breakfast.

The fact of Jesus' birth is undeniable. What interpretation we put on that birth is open to question. There are major difficulties, the main one being the passage of time. Can you remember what lead up to a recent argument you had with your spouse? Can you remember with certainty who said what? There is difficulty in establishing with certainty the facts, let alone the interpretation that could be placed on them.

Z: I think it's safest if you just say that Lucy was right.

Whether my interpretation is the 'right' one is not only a matter of faith but, more importantly, is it open to scrutiny? Does it make sense in the light of all my other experiences? Is it compatible with what I know of God as revealed in the bible? There is something called the Methodist quadrilateral.

Z: Are you getting mathematical again?

It is simply the suggestion that we discern a point of view by referring to four things; the bible, reason, tradition and experience. Does what I am saying, and believing, make sense in the light of these four points of reference?

Does it make any sense at all? These are questions for discernment and we look at that topic in chapter nine for the moment the question arises as to whether we are free and if so, in what sense.

## Points to Ponder:

1. Who is God for you?

2. What difference does your belief in God make to the way you live your life?

3. What would your world be like without your Christian faith?

4. In what ways could you describe yourself as an atheist?

5. In what ways might a Christian life be different to a non Christian life?

## Meditation:

Take time to relax. Sit in a comfortable position. Find that quiet place within you. Become aware of your breathing. Don't adjust your breathing, just breathe normally, no stress or strain.

If you find yourself distracted by external noises or internal thoughts, quietly focus again on your breathing. God is closer to you than your own breathing.

Continue for at least ten minutes.

## References

1. Robinson John A.T., <u>Honest to God</u> , SCM, 1965, p.47
2. ibid. p.55
3. ibid.
4. Robinson John A.T., <u>Exploration into God,</u> SCM, 1965, p.55
5. Jüngel, Eberhard, <u>God as the Mystery of the World</u>, T & T Clark 1977, p.7
6. Simon, U.E. <u>A Theology of Auschwitz.</u> Gollancz, 1967
7. Zahrnt, H, <u>The Question of God</u>, Collins, 1969
8. Bonhoeffer, Dietrich, <u>Letters and Papers from Prison</u>, Fontana, 1965, p.91

9.  Robinson, John A.T., <u>The New Reformation?</u>, SCM, 1965, p.106ff

10. Weatherhead, Leslie D., <u>The Christian Agnostic</u>, Hodder & Stoughton, 1965

11. <u>The New Reformation?</u> op cit., p.113

12. Young, Wm Paul, <u>The Shack</u>, Hodder, 2007

13. Bonhoeffer, op. cit., p.123

14. Moltmann, Jürgen, <u>The Crucified God</u>, SCM, 1974

15. Jüngel, op. cit., p.13

16. Rothwell, Malcolm, <u>Journeying with God</u>, Epworth, 2001

17. Holloway, Richard, <u>Dancing on the Edge</u>, Fount, 1997, p.44

18. Jüngel, op. cit.

19. <u>The Cloud of Unknowing</u>, penguin classics, 1961, p.59f

20. Barry, William A., <u>Spiritual Direction and the Encounter with God</u>, Paulist    Press,    1992, p.27

21. ibid., p.29

22. ibid., p.31

23. ibid., p.30

# Chapter 8

## FREEDOM TO DECIDE?

Sometimes I go shopping in our local supermarket and I am usually overwhelmed by the huge number of choices. The new shopping centres are built like cathedrals and choice is the God to be worshipped. People shop for hours making choices about clothes, games, food, holidays, furniture, almost for the sake of it. This is so called retail therapy. There are many decisions to make but are they really important? There are choices to be made even for the simplest of items. One no longer buys a loaf of bread pure and simple. One has to decide whether it is sliced or not, small or large, thin, thick or medium sliced, whole meal or granary, white or brown, ordinary or slim line, healthy eating or not etc. This is just for one item on a very long list! Shopping can take a long time.

Z: I've noticed you spend a lot of time in front of the chocolate biscuits.

Yes, I'm afraid that when it comes to chocolate, resistance is futile. However, choosing bread may seem a trivial example but it does illustrate that everyday all of us are involved in making choices. Even at the beginning of the day I have to decide whether to get up or stay in bed, whether to have a shower or a wash or not bother with either, what to wear and whether to eat any breakfast and, if so, what I am going to eat and drink. All this in the first few minutes of the day!! We need to insert the caveat that there are some things over which we have no choice – for example, when and where we are born, who our parents are and our genetic makeup.

Of course, some choices are less important than others. It doesn't really matter whether I decide to wear my red chequered socks, my plain black ones, or those emblazoned with the words 'not socks again'.

Z: It is very important to me which socks I wear.

On the other hand some choices are literally life changing. Shall I marry or not and if the right partner comes along shall we have children or not? There are other serious career choices to be made as well. Do I follow my heart's desire and become a priest or missionary even though there is no money in it or shall I forgo that desire and follow a career that earns me far more money and lots of prestige and status?

You may well argue that this is all very well but what about those who have no choice. Millions of people in the world are faced with issues of survival and that alone. There are no fancy decisions to be taken; only where is the next meal coming from and where do I get clean water from? Approximately 30,000 people die needlessly everyday because of poverty. That is the equivalent of a tsunami every nine days. More than half the world's population lives on just over £1 per day.

We in the so-called developed world have to live with these horrendous figures and gaunt faces which often appear on our television screens. We live in the comfort zone and wonder at our complicity in a consumer society. Are we culpable? Enmeshed? Ashamed? Indifferent? Apathetic? Powerless? Have I in any way contributed to the universal predicament? By the choice I have made could it be that I buy food without a thought of where it comes from, or clothes without a thought of the cheap labour that is involved in its manufacture. Does my life style involve making a large contribution to my carbon footprint? Maybe I indulge in frequent cheap weekend flights or lots of car driving when walking would be a better, and certainly, healthier option. In many ways, we in the West are being challenged to the core of our being to make choices that do not harm the planet or contribute to the poverty of other human beings.

Any choice that I make presupposes that I am free to make that choice. Am I really free or have I been so conditioned by my early upbringing and cultural experiences that the whole idea of being free is an illusion? I am certainly constrained to a certain extent by my genes. My temperament and talents have been set within a given physiological framework. As Rousseau famously said, 'Man is born free, and everywhere he is in chains.' I was born into a Methodist family and going to church was part of my upbringing and therefore becoming a Methodist minister was not a complete surprise, especially as my uncle was a Methodist minister. If I had been born in Outer Mongolia I would probably have spent my days as a nomad in the Steppes of Russia with a completely different life to the one that I now have.

Z: Somehow I can't quite see you as a wandering nomad. You are too fond of your own bed.

Not only have I been affected by my early upbringing but

there are forces at play which, by definition, I know nothing about. Freud is the person who really began the study of the unconscious and he noted that even an apparent everyday occurrence such as a so-called slip of the tongue can have an unconscious motivation.

More importantly, the structure of our brain and central nervous system affects our behaviour. These are the biological bases of behaviour. Cognitive processes such as learning, remembering and perceiving are dependent on a fully functioning cerebral cortex and central nervous system. In the early days of psychiatry, invasive surgery which entailed the removal of the prefrontal lobes was one way of dealing with particular kinds of mental illness. Lesions in other parts of the brain can affect aggressive behaviour or the sexual drive. Details are not important. Suffice it to say that modifications in the structure of the brain affect behaviour. This is beyond question.

Z: Does this mean I can't help being a clown?

It probably does. Chemical changes also affect the brain and therefore behaviour. Drugs, medically prescribed or otherwise, can affect us, as can caffeine, nicotine and alcohol. More recently, geneticists are increasingly finding particular genes for particular illnesses. Will a gene be found to suggest that a person is more likely to become a criminal than a policeman? If that were the case, where does that leave the important principle of free will? This is not a new question. Common sense dictates that we all have an element of free choice and we exercise this regularly. Nevertheless, some psychologists adopt a deterministic principle and all students of psychology soon become aware of experiments which indicate the effects of early upbringing and the importance of physiological and biochemical factors in behaviour.

Z: I have a funny feeling you are going to get psychological.

I'm afraid so Zeno; you might want to miss the next part because it gets a bit technical. My feeling is that we all think that we have lots of freedom and I'm not at all sure that is true.

Psychologists are agreed that much of our behaviour is conditioned. Pavlov and his dogs demonstrated classical conditioning. The dogs were trained to salivate at the sound of a bell because the bell had become associated with the presentation of food. Pavlov considered that learning occurred if a neutral stimulus, in this case a bell, and an unconditioned stimulus, in this case salivation, were paired. Humans can start to feel hungry at a certain time if they are used to having a meal at that time even if, physiologically, they are not hungry. They have no choice in the matter. The unconditioned response has become a conditioned response. Of course, there is always the choice of whether to eat or not.

Z: My trouble is I always seem to feel hungry.

You would! Operant conditioning, on the other hand, works through a system of reinforcement or reward but the receipt of this reward is dependent on an appropriate response being made. In the case of classical conditioning the appropriate response is elicited and the learner has no choice in making the response since it is involuntary; but in operant conditioning the responses are emitted voluntarily and the problem for the learner is to select the appropriate response from the several possibilities. An early experiment was by

Thorndike who tested how animals like cats learn to escape from a 'puzzle box'. Initially, the cat has no idea how to escape and its behaviour is random. Eventually the cat discovers it can escape by pressing a lever. The cat has been rewarded by pressing the lever; it has escaped and thus the lever could be denoted as a positive reinforcer because freedom has been attained. In other typical experiments pellets of food are offered to hungry rats when they learn to press a lever. Lever pressing is the required response and is said to be an operant response because the animal has learned to operate on its environment. In this case the food has become the positive reinforcer.

Humans are quite used to positive reinforcement. This can come in the form of praise, pocket money, being given some kind of special treat or whatever.

Z: All I need is for people to laugh.

Children soon learn that the desired behaviour brings its own rewards. We are all socially conditioned to behave in certain ways; so called anti-social behaviour is frowned upon and discouraged. Discomforting situations are normally aversive and punishing, for example, when we are told off, or love is withheld or we are 'grounded'. Such reinforcements are called negative in that they discourage certain kinds of behaviour. Negative reinforcers are called aversive in the sense that they are the things organisms turn away from.

Z: I suppose 'hell fire' preaching would come under this category, as would dear old uncle George who you mentioned in the last chapter.

Yes they would. Skinner was an arch proponent of operant conditioning and more generally he was known for his investigations into the factors which control behaviour. Years ago he wrote 'escape and avoidance play a much more important role in the struggle for freedom when the aversive conditions are generated by other people.' (1) We all tend to avoid other people when they are rude, or irritating or just generally annoying. In many ways other people can also be intentionally aversive. Thus a parent nags a child until a job is done. The child performs the tasks and escapes the nagging, and, incidentally, reinforces the parent's behaviour. Skinner says that 'in one form or another intentional aversive control is the pattern of most social coordination – in ethics, religions, government, economics, education, psychotherapy, and family life.

(2)

Z: Are you saying that we are not as free as we think we are?

We are all conditioned or controlled to a certain extent by different patterns of reinforcement. For example, the national lottery is an obvious form of an interval schedule of reinforcement. The reward is certainly not contingent on any work done by the gambler and the success comes after variable intervals of time. The gambler is kept on course in the belief that next time the reward might arrive. A reinforcement pattern known as variable ratio is at the heart of other gambling systems. For example, a casino pays people for giving it money, that is, it pays them when they make bets. But it pays on a kind of schedule that sustains betting even though, in the long run, the amount paid is less than the amount wagered.

Z: It's all very clever. People are persuaded to keep on gambling because next time they might just be lucky.

For Skinner the control of behaviour is entirely desirable. 'What we need is a technology of behaviour. For example, we could solve our problems quickly enough if we could adjust the growth of the world's population as precisely as we adjust the course of a space-ship'. But, my guess is that many are more than a little uncomfortable with this suggestion. Although, in China, population has been restricted to one child per couple there is a perception that this is taking too much freedom away from individuals and giving too much control to the State. In England there is often a vehement defence of the right to be free so long as actions take place within the law.. As a result, by insisting on such things as freedom of speech, a minimum of censorship, and a fear of the nanny state we have laid ourselves open to commercial exploitation. Such commodities as alcohol, tobacco and entertainment have been given until recently an almost free rein.

Although there is a nine o'clock watershed on television, because of the multi-channels now available and the ease with which programmes can be recorded, children are free to watch almost any kind of programme. There is also a wide accessibility of all kinds of material on the internet. Only recently has the state thought about restricting the use of chat rooms and porn sites and has actually intervened to stop smoking in public places. At present, there is some lobbying to restrict the sale of alcohol because this is seen as one of the main contributors to crime. There has been a great deal of debate on the issue of how long potential terrorist suspects should be imprisoned for without being charged and without infringing their basic human rights.

Z: I can see how external controls impinge on our freedom, and how necessary some of those controls are but what about inner, personal freedom?

That is a very good question and there are many more. Are we free to do exactly what we want when we want? If we are not free where does that leave the question of moral responsibility? If I am a pre programmed machine I cannot be held responsible for any of my actions. As the lyric in West Side story goes.....................

Dear kindly Judge, your Honour,My parents treat me rough.With all their marijuana,They won't give me a puff. They didn't wanna have me,But somehow I was had.Leapin' lizards! That's why I'm so bad!

Thus, the singing teenager opts out of his individual responsibility because it is all the fault of his parents.

Z: Yep. Just blame it on Mum and Dad.

I have personally seen many people for counselling who have been greatly affected by their early experiences. The most dramatic example of this is the person who has been permanently scarred by being abused as a small child. The person grows up into an adult with a deep, deep feeling of mistrust of others, a huge amount of anger and an acute inner pain which is like a wrench tearing at their inside. Thankfully not all have such dramatic and heartbreaking experiences but, nevertheless, many people grow into adults with a deep feeling of low self-esteem. They have feelings of worthlessness, of being unable to accept themselves. There is a chorus of negative voices singing loudly with them. They try to escape from these voices by seeking different relationships, bigger and better houses, more exotic holidays, job promotion and so on but the voices always remain. Another escape is to deny them by becoming overbearing or arrogant. Again the voices remain.

Of course, these feelings of not being good enough often come from early childhood where a parent can often exhort their child to do better. Even if they have achieved 99% in a test they want to know why their offspring has not done better. Then there are the conditions which parents put on their children, for example, I will love you but only if you behave in a certain way.

The psychotherapist, Carl Rogers, developed the technique of person-centred therapy in which his main tenet was that the basic condition for a healthy person is the experience of unconditional love. This non-judgemental, positive regard became the basis for his therapeutic relationships. As noted above, most of us do not experience this unconditional love. There are usually strings attached. Rogers therefore struggles with the conflict between determinism and freedom. 'As we enter this field of psychotherapy with objective research methods, we are, like any other scientist, committed to a complete determinism. From this point of view every thought, feeling, and action of the client is determined by what preceded it. There can be no such thing as freedom'. (3)

Z: Help! Am I just a robot?

That is precisely the dilemma for Rogers because people often feel within themselves the power of naked choice and so are patently not robots. He overcomes the dilemma by describing what he calls the fully functioning person. This kind of person is more able to live with all their feelings and reactions and is more aware of them. On the other hand another person may be much more defensive and not be able to move in the direction they would like to. They are determined by factors outside of their control. 'The fully functioning person…not only experiences, but utilizes, the most absolute freedom when he spontaneously, freely, and voluntarily chooses and wills that which is also absolutely determined.' (4) The therapeutic process is that which enables a person to free themselves from those things that hold them back and prevent a free choice.

The strictly determinist view was adopted, not surprisingly, by the psychoanalyst Freud, and by the behaviourist psychologist mentioned above, Skinner. Determinism is the belief that every single event has a cause, and that every event is completely determined by its causes. Science itself proceeds along these very same lines. The created world follows certain laws and therefore we can predict future events. For example, we can predict when the next eclipse will occur and we can plot with amazing accuracy a rocket's path to a distant planet. A determinist would say that human behaviour follows certain laws and can therefore also be predicted. This would certainly be Skinner's view. However, it does contain an inherent piece of illogic. The implication is that Skinner himself was not free to develop his theories or express his views. Are his views merely the result of his early conditioning and upbringing? Are his writings the result of an irresistible urge and if so, are there any criteria for deciding whether he is right or wrong?

Z: I am getting well out of my comfort zone but I think I have heard of something in science called the uncertainty principle.

Yes indeed, science is not as certain and deterministic as people think. There is a degree of uncertainty. Heisenberg discovered the principle which states that it is impossible to measure the position and the velocity of a particle at the same time, because measuring one changes the other. The observer cannot be separated from that which is observed. Furthermore, the behaviour of individual particles is unpredictable. In this sense determinism is well and truly dead.

Z: Thank goodness for that but does this apply to people? Aren't we absolutely determined by our genes?

Interesting work is being done at the moment with identical twins.

Z: I thought all twins were identical.

Not at all. Identical twins appear when a fertilised egg splits into two a few days after conception. This means that identical twins have exactly the same genetic makeup. Fraternal twins, on the other hand, appear when two different eggs are fertilised at the same time. By studying identical twins researchers hope to discover the effect of environmental factors.

Z: The old nature versus nurture controversy.

Exactly. Why is it that in a pair of identical twins one develops leukaemia and the other doesn't, or one becomes much more obese than the other, or one is heterosexual whilst the other is homosexual? The research is in its early stages but it seems that an environmental factor has the ability to trigger a certain gene. For example in the first case above one twin had tonsillitis. Perhaps this switched a gene into the on position and leukaemia developed.

Z: To put it very simply, we are not solely determined by our genes, what happens in our lives has an effect.

Exactly. In the second case above, one twin led a much more active and outgoing life style, whereas the other sat at a desk all day and had an unhealthy diet. Consequently, in spite of their identical genes, they grew with different physiques.

Z: I'm beginning to feel more optimistic about my own freedom.

A more extreme version of determinism is fatalism. This is the belief that all future events are mapped out and nothing you can do will alter your fate. What ever will be will be. A theological version of this is the doctrine of predestination, the notion that we are elected and chosen by God and our future is mapped out. It is one thing to say that freedom is limited but quite another to say that we don't have any at all.

Z: But what about God's will? Don't you pray 'thy will be done' in the Lord's prayer?

Yes we do. Certainly Jesus thought that God has a will. He says in the fourth gospel, 'My food is to obey the will of him who sent me and to complete his work.' (John 4: 34) There are also the words of Jesus in the garden of Gethsemane, 'Father, all things are possible; remove this cup from me; yet, not what I want, but what you want.' (Mark 14:36) Older versions have 'not what I will, but what you will.' The implication is that Jesus always sought to follow the will of God.

Problems arise when it is assumed that God's will is fixed and final rather like the script of a play. All Christians have to do, it is assumed, is to learn the lines, so to speak, and everything will be all right. The will of God is thought to be a blueprint which has been planned for each of us. This can produce great difficulty for the believer who tries to discover the lines, learn them and then suffers pangs of guilt or remorse if it is thought that the lines they have learnt are not the correct ones. Furthermore this scenario implies that God's will is intransigent and that God only has one will.

Z: Where would that leave human freedom?

Where indeed? Where does it leave our ability to discern? God does not have a blueprint that we must all slavishly follow. 'God's will for us is that we should learn to respond in freedom to God's love for us, and to give shape to our individual and common lives in freedom by the choices that we make.' (5) Let me give you an illustration.

Z: That would help

I love my family and I sometimes have ideas about what I would like them to be. However, there is no way, at least no loving way, in which I can force them to be a teacher, a doctor, a plumber or to marry, or to have a family or whatever. My only loving desire is that they lead happy, fulfilled lives and achieve their potential. Within that desire there are all sorts of possibilities. This means that predicting future behaviour is very difficult

Under certain tightly controlled conditions it may be possible to not only predict but actually manipulate another's behaviour. This could occur in penal institutions or mental hospitals where inmates are fairly well controlled but even here there are some unpredictable outcomes. The film 'One flew over the cuckoo's nest' would be a good example of a patient being forced to conform to the regime but in the end behaving in unpredictable ways. In the film the patient struggles to change his behaviour and become free of constraints.

Z: So there can be surprises. That's a relief. I wonder if God is ever surprised. If he knows everything that is going to happen he can't be surprised. How boring!

My family sometimes say to me 'Dad, you are so predictable!'

Z: You are. Very boring.

On the other hand there is the possibility that they will say 'that was a complete surprise, we didn't know you had it in you'. This however is not quite the point. To predict somebody else's behaviour precisely would require a detailed knowledge of their brain state at any one time. This is highly unlikely given the complexity of the brain. It is however even more complicated because our mental activity is also governed by the particular environmental context we find ourselves in. The conclusion is that an expert in brain science may be able to predict, in principle, a person's behaviour but the person himself remains free.

Is it possible for a person to predict their own behaviour? This is even more difficult and, logically, impossible. If someone knows their own mental activity which might give rise to a certain behaviour, as soon as they knew that mental activity it would alter it and therefore the predicted activity would change. Hypothetically this would mean that if we knew the brain state of Bill Bobbins then we could predict his behaviour. Whether we know the brain state of somebody or not, and it is highly unlikely that we could ever fully know it in all its complexity, nevertheless we can often predict how somebody will behave.

Z: Has it taken you all this time to come to the conclusion that we are free but not as much as we might think?

The whole concept of free-will is highly complex and philosophers have debated it for years. The major point is that if there is no such thing as free-will then where does that leave the question of moral choice? If we are predetermined how can we be responsible for any choices that we make? Moreover, 'so long as people go on having to make up their minds what to do, they will have need of principles ( including moral principles) to help them to do it'. (6)

Z: That's a relief. I need all the help I can get.

Clearly, the question as to whether we have the freedom to make a choice is highly complex and a short chapter hardly pays it any justice. Another strand to the question is where is God in all this? A Christian obviously believes in the existence of God, but more than that, we are affected by the grace of God. A believer's behaviour is also affected by prayer, meditation, worship and the like, it is not simply determined in a mechanistic kind of way but the belief is that God has a hand in their lives. Indeed, the belief is that God wants people to have and to enjoy their freedom. With regard to physical freedom the central event of the Old Testament is about the liberation of the children of Israel from slavery in Egypt. In the Exodus, God delivered the children of Israel. They were set free. Freedom resulted from the action of God. It brought the Israelites into a new relationship with God.

Z: What about the New Testament? Is physical freedom an

issue there? I thought slavery was quite common in the New Testament.

Quite right, moreover, no New Testament writer actually speaks against slavery. That was left for Wilberforce nearly eighteen hundred years later. The various texts about freedom in the New Testament are about inner freedom and about the relationship a Christian has with God.

you will know the truth, and the truth will make you free.
(John 8:32)
so if the Son makes you free, you will be free indeed.
(John 8: 36)

This means that if we open ourselves to the Spirit of God then we can discern and see the truth at a particular moment and be set free of, for example, a particular prejudice that we have held on to. In a very real sense we are all enslaved, to fame or beauty, or to unfulfilled desires, or to alcohol, or to a particular behaviour pattern or to whatever.

Z: In your case it is probably chocolate.

I am not admitting to anything. Slavery occurs when we are robbed of our freedom. It fences us in so there are no choices to make. This can actually happen in the church. There can be strong expectations, often unspoken, to behave in certain ways but:-

where the Spirit of the Lord is, there is freedom.
(2 Cor. 3:17)
for freedom, Christ has set us free. Stand firm, therefore, and do not submit again to a yoke of slavery. (Gal. 5:1)

The irony is that Paul talks about Christians being slaves but the difference is that this is a slavery that we choose.
you have been freed from sin and enslaved to God.
(Roms. 6:22)
Of course, none of us is fully free and that is why Paul also talks about hoping and waiting with 'eager longing.'
(Roms. 8: 19)

Christian discipleship, then, is about inner freedom, but this is not anarchy. Far from it.

Z: You mean I can't do just what I want to do?

In a way, yes. It is 'eternal truth' number 41 in a book by Kopp. 'You are free to do whatever you like. You need only face the consquences.' (7) All our actions influence the future, no matter how small we think they are.

Z: Is that what's called the butterfly effect?

Precisely. Therefore we can only talk about responsible freedom. Sometimes it is hard work to choose. It can be very tempting to opt out and let others choose for us. 'Oh, I don't mind,' 'anything will do,' 'I'm not fussy'. Sometimes it is not important but at other times, by refusing to accept our own responsibility, we let the forces of evil take over.

Z: Ah yes, as you said earlier, 'all that is needed for evil to triumph is for good people to do nothing'.

It is more than that. Christian discipleship carries with it certain constraints. How do I spend my money, my time and so on? Is it important or not whether I buy fairly traded goods, accumulate air miles so I can fly long distances, or recycle as much as possible? Sometimes we can be a prisoner of other people's expectations of us. There is a deep inner need to conform and not stand out against the flow. However, the Christian life is not about doing just what I want, when I want, it involves being aware of the effects of my actions on other people. This brings us on to the question of discernment.

## Points to Ponder:

1. How free do you feel?

2. What could you do to increase your freedom?

3. In what way is being a slave of God the same as being free? Does the idea of freedom contradict being a slave to God?

4. Someone once said 'love God and do what you will'. How can that be true?

5. What choices have you made today? How do you feel about the decisions you have taken?

## Meditation:

We come with self-inflicted pains
Of broken trust and chosen wrong,
Half-free, half-bound by inner chains,
By social forces swept along,
By powers and systems close confined,
Yet seeking hope for humankind. (8)

# References

1. Skinner, B.F., <u>Beyond Freedom and Dignity</u>, Pelican, 1979, p. 32
2. ibid. p 33
3. Roger, Carl R., <u>On Becoming A Person</u>, Constable, 1988, p.192
4. ibid., p. 193
5. Lonsdale, David, <u>Eyes To See, Ears To Hear</u>, DLT., p.65
6. Hare, R.M., <u>Freedom And Reason</u>, OUP, 1972, p.63
7. Kopp, Sheldon B., <u>If you meet the Buddha on the road, kill him!</u>, Bantam, 1972. p.224
8. Hymns & Psalms number 500

# Chapter 9

## DISCERNMENT

The prerequisite for Christian discernment is that it takes place within the context of prayer. The Spiritual Exercises of Ignatius offer precisely such a context. Prayer in the sense of being present to God and listening to what God has to say in the things that happen to us, in the people we meet and in the silence. I fear that too often our prayers are quite different to the boy Samuel who said, 'Speak, Lord, for your servant listens.' (1Sam. 3:10) All too often our prayers are, 'Listen, Lord, for your servant speaks.'(1) We are too concerned about what we can bring to God but the reality is that we can bring nothing to God. 'Prayer is not something we give to God; it is rather the opening of our heart so that God can give himself to us.' (2)

Prayer is being present and available for God and this requires a degree of humility. How can we truly be open to God if we are so full of ourselves and our own importance, or, on the other hand, riddled with self-doubt? Humility is not about feeling inferior but is about being 'without pretence, down to earth'. (3) Humility involves an awareness of who we are before God, accepting all the parts of ourselves so that we become fully integrated and whole as human beings.

It is therefore recognising our own shortcomings but also recognising the gifts and contributions others can make.

In the process of discernment the object is to discover God's will but it is not to discover that will for the whole of one's life but simply for a given situation. Discernment is for a particular individual in a particular situation, given their individual gifts, personality, temperament, character, and circumstances.

The process of discernment is carried out in a setting which presupposes God's love. It is assumed that the 'voice of God' is calling for a free, personal response. The person is free to do or not to do what God prefers. Any choice, of course, in this context is between two morally acceptable courses of action. ( #170, see note 4)

Another way of putting this is that the process involves looking for the insights and movements that lead to a more authentic life style. Where is your deepest self engaged? What is it that brings you to life? Where is the fount of your energy? It was the genius of Ignatius to discover the link between making a choice and discerning the movement of spirits within. This was a major discovery when he was shot by a cannonball.

Z: Did you say canon ball?

Yes. When Ignatius was 26 years old, his patron fell on hard times for disobeying the new king Emperor Charles V. Ignatius soon found himself serving as a soldier. Four years later in 1521, he found himself at Pamplona, facing the French invaders. A cannonball seriously injured his leg.

He was well treated by the French but he required two operations on his leg. In fact, a third one was necessary because he was still unable to wear the close fitting tights that were then fashionable for men. This third operation Ignatius deliberately chose.

Z: He must have had a very high pain threshold.

Indeed. There were no anaesthetics. During a long convalescence, he began to read the only books that were available. These were not romantic novels, as he would have wished but The Life of Christ and The Lives of the Saints. This convalescence became the first major turning point in his life. Instead of dreaming about becoming a great warrior and winning the hand of some fair lady he began to dream about following Christ in great hardship. He discovered that the latter dreams gave him a feeling of contentment whereas the former dreams of deeds of chivalry left him sad and discontented. The conclusion that Ignatius drew from this was that the dreams of Christ were inspired by God whereas the other dreams were not. Ignatius used the terminology of good and bad spirits. It has been argued that it was this discernment of different spirits that began his conversion. Today we would probably talk about different feelings rather than different spirits.

In brief Ignatius began to feel that Jesus Christ as a King with a Kingdom was far more important than the Spanish King and his kingdom whom he had been serving. Moreover, he had been greatly moved by the lives of the Saints he had been reading about. He found them to be brave and marvellous people and he wanted to be a follower of Christ in the Spirit of the Saints. Out of the crucible of his own experience

Ignatius developed his Spiritual Exercises and they begin with the 'First Principle and Foundation.'

'...we must make ourselves indifferent to all created things, as far as we are allowed free choice.....consequently, as far as we are concerned, we should not prefer health to sickness, riches to poverty, honour to dishonour, a long life to a short life.... our one desire and choice should be what is more conducive to the end for which we are created.' ( 5)

Z: Hang on minute. I would much prefer a young and healthy life and I wouldn't mind being a bit richer.

Let me explain. Firstly, Ignatius clearly assumes that some freedom is a given in the Christian life and that choices can therefore be made. A key word is 'indifference.' The problem is that the word has all sorts of negative connotations like apathy or 'I couldn't care less.' In the Ignatian sense it does not mean this. Nor does it mean being indifferent to people or that we should be unfeeling and unresponsive people and certainly it is not about being indifferent to evil. It means being open to all possibilities so that God can draw us to where God wants us to be. We can only be where God wants us to be if we are truly indifferent. Ignatius's own description of indifference is 'as a balance at equilibrium, without leaning to one side or the other.' (#15) In other words it is about cultivating a sense of poise so that we are ready to go in the direction that God indicates. It is this indifference which is crucial in any consideration of freedom or the desire to do God's will.

Z: If God has a will – as you discussed in chapter three.

Quite so. Here I am using the phrase as short hand for getting in touch with the direction God would like us to take.

Ignatius says that we must be indifferent even to those things that are close to our biological and psychological make-up. That is why we should not prefer health to sickness and so on. The idea is rather like the Methodist covenant service which contains the words 'Put me to what you will, rank me with whom you will; put me to doing, put me to suffering' (6) and is very similar to what Paul asserts in his letter to the Philippians. (Phil. 4:11-13)

Z: I still find it a strange idea. Surely people would want to be healthy rather than sick.

Of course, the idea runs counter to the values of the world. There is often a tension between the values of this world and the perspective of God. However, God loves all equally. God is impartial to whether people are healthy, educated, young or old. God has no favourites. God is indifferent.

But I agree with you. Any "normal" person would prefer the reverse of these values, that is, health to sickness, riches to poverty and so on. Indeed we are urged to lead healthy lives and to attain wealth in one way or another and then we will indeed be truly happy. The problem is that these attainments become addictions or obsessions and we lose our inner freedom. These attainments become 'attachments' and so in discerning a way forward we often present God with a list of conditions. 'I will be happy to work wherever you want me to Lord just as long as I am near my ageing parents, my children are near a good school, the house is in a good neighbourhood and it is not too far away from Bolton because I support Bolton Wanderers.'

Z: Are you their only supporter?

Very funny. De Mello writes 'an attachment is a belief that

without something you are not going to be happy.' (7) It is very similar to desire or craving and whilst these feelings prevail there is no possibility of attaining indifference and therefore it is very difficult for effective discernment to take place. As de Mello writes 'attachments are blind. Clinging, craving, and desire are blind.' (8) He defines love as 'the dropping of all attachments. It is only when I cease to cling to you, to need you, to possess you that I can begin to love you.........Love requires freedom, and freedom is lost in the attachment.' (9)

Z: OK. Suppose I am in that rarefied place of having dropped my attachments. I am 'poised' and in a place of prayer. You have still not said anything about how I can actually discern a way forward.

The first way is when we are, as it were, 'zapped'. The decision seems to come out of nowhere but we know for sure that it is the will of God. We know that we have been touched by God.

It happened on a Sunday morning, the last day of a weekend retreat. John had visited the chapel. As he knelt down he experienced a powerful shock – like a bolt of lightning. He felt his whole being lifted up. He had to say "yes". He had to enter the ministry. He had no control over it. All he could do was go with it. There were no arguments, no doubts. It was decided. There was total certainty that God has spoken. He experienced a great sense of peace, joy and direction. He knew he had been chosen by God.

One could argue that St. Matthew and St. Paul were called in this particular way. They had no doubts that God was calling them to follow him. This is a depth of experience, which the soul cannot reach by its own efforts. It comes across as utterly convincing and compelling and carries with it a rightness that cannot be challenged. There is an absolute certainty and clarity around the choice. Of course there is the need to take the experience to God in prayer to gain confirmation.

Z: I think I am more likely to get zapped by a custard pie.

The second way is very much based on the conviction that God communicates through our feelings. All discernment involves feelings but in this method there is a special focus on our affective states and our cognitive processes are brought to bear to evaluate these feelings. In Ignatian terms this is his "discernment of Spirits" and involves noting the significant changes or movements in the feelings which are associated with a particular course of action or actions. Through those observations the hope is that one can discern the activity of God and the forces which may be resisting it.

The two words, which Ignatius frequently uses in this context, are 'consolation' and 'desolation'. During this second method of discernment 'much light and understanding are derived through experience of desolations and consolations and discernment of diverse spirits'. (#176 also see p,316-317) The feelings are to do with whether a person is experiencing a movement towards God or a movement away from God. In consolation the experience is of being drawn closer to God so that we are less self-centred and more open to others. Typical feelings associated with this experience are joyful awareness, a sense of gratitude, a state of peace and so on. 'The main feature of them is that their direction is towards growth, creativity and a genuine fullness of life and love in that they draw us to a fuller, effective, generous love of God and other people, and to a right love of ourselves.'(10) These are pleasant feelings of joy, peace and delight in the love of God and being a disciple of Jesus. Sometimes these feelings seem to come, as it were, out of nowhere, and without any apparent cause.

Z: A nice warm glow.

Yes but feelings of consolation can be deceptive. It is part of our human nature to be resistant to the Spirit of God. 'It is characteristic of the Evil One to fight against such happiness and consolation by proposing fallacious reasoning, subtleties, and continual deceptions.' (# 329) People can be lead astray by apparent good.

Ignatius gives rules, which outline the dangers. (# 329-336) One possible indication of danger is that good suggestions are often far-fetched, for example, a newcomer to Christianity may be directed to organise a mission to Mongolia. A key test is whether the resulting decision draws the person away from Christ or closer to Christ. Even when there is consolation without previous cause there is need to carefully assess what follows in the after-glow. 'We must carefully assess the whole course of our thoughts' and see if these thoughts 'terminate in something evil, or distracting, or less good than the soul had formerly proposed to do'. (#332) These thoughts are the cognitive signs of a deceptive good.

A further test that Ignatius gives is that 'in souls that are progressing to greater perfection, the action of the good angel is delicate, gentle, delightful. It may be compared to a drop of water penetrating a sponge. The action of the evil spirit upon such souls is violent, noisy, and disturbing. It may be compared to a drop of water falling upon a stone.' (#335) If the experience is producing great trouble, disturbance and turmoil rather than peace and tranquillity, serious questions have to be raised.

Z: Maybe it is more like dropping a stone in a bucket of water.

That would certainly produce turbulence. Feelings of desolation are the complete opposite of feelings of consolation and involve restlessness, inner darkness, failure, guilt and life ceases to have meaning. 'Their characteristic tendency is to draw us away from God and things which have to do with God, and lead us to be self-centred, closed in and unconcerned about God or other people.' (11) These are unpleasant feelings but are not necessarily destructive. Ignatius writes that these experiences can be occasions for growth if dealt with correctly. (#318-322) However, it is very important that decisions are not made when we are in a time of desolation, precisely because such decisions could be destructive and lead us away from God. (#318) For example, it is not usually a good idea to make a major decision when suffering a bereavement. Furthermore 'though in desolation, we must never change our former resolutions.' (#319) Indeed the suggestion is that we act against the desolation by intensifying our prayer, meditation and self-examination.

Z: Can you give an example?

Janet has been a church lay worker for a number of years and her work is greatly valued. However, she has recently been asked about a ministry in the diaconate. She feels attracted to the presbyteral ministry and has the gifts necessary but wonders whether it is the right time. With the help of her spiritual director she tries to discern God's will for her by using this second mode of Ignatian discernment. She tries to discern her dispositions, whether they be attractions or aversions, when she considers before God her experiences as a lay worker. She follows the same process when she considers the possibility of being a presbyteral minister. Time is spent in prayer trying to be indifferent to either position and seeking only to do God's will. The process of discernment is a matter of sifting through the various feelings and discovering those, which bring desolation, and those, which bring consolation. For discernment the crucial question is in which direction the feelings are leading. What is the affective movement? Ignatius gives further rules for the discernment of spirits (#329-336) and especially highlights the fact that sometimes consolation can be false. Though good in themselves the experiences may be drawing us away from something better. In colourful language he compares the 'enemy ....in his manner of acting to a false lover. He seeks to remain hidden and does not want to be discovered.' (#326) In these cases Ignatius gives two pieces of advice. Firstly we must trace back from the harmful experience to the time when things started to go wrong (#333-334) and secondly tell somebody what is happening. (#326)

Because there is such a thing as false consolation, false joy and peace, a basic method of discernment is to note the final result. One thing to do is to examine the whole course of our thoughts. 'If the beginning and middle and end of the course of thoughts are wholly good and directed to what is entirely right, it is a sign that they are from the good angel.' (#333) If the course of our thoughts terminates in something evil or something that causes a disturbance or disquiet, this is a 'clear sign that the thoughts are proceeding from the evil spirit.' (ibid)

Z: This is all very well but it seems to depend a lot on feelings.

It does indeed and the trouble is that many people, especially men, are not in touch with their feelings.

Z: That is a very sexist comment.

I'm afraid it is. I remember quite clearly going onto a counselling course when I was in my early thirties. The question I was asked, along with other course members, was 'how are you feeling?' The honest answer was that I had no idea!! – at my age!! I had learned how to play the game of our educational system. If you wanted to get anywhere you had to pass tests and examinations and for that you had to learn facts, not feelings. What an indictment of our educational system that feelings are completely ignored. This is even more of a problem for males because our culture is such that 'little boys don't cry' and real men exhibit a 'stiff upper lip.' There are signs that it is more acceptable for men not only to acknowledge they have feelings but also to actually express them. For example, football can be a very macho game but there have been recent instances of well known footballers crying in public. Of course our feelings have to be checked out by our thinking otherwise we would be a prey to whatever we were feeling.

Z: Even I know it's not a good idea to jump into bed with someone just because you like them. Is there a method of discernment which is not quite so dependent on feelings?

The third method of discernment is during a time of tranquillity. It takes place in the context of considering first the purpose for which we are born 'that is, for the praise of God our Lord and for the salvation of our soul.' (#177) Ignatius now gives two ways, from this beginning, for determining a choice. The first way can seem to be very rational.

Basically it is to have in mind the action about which a choice is to be made and then listing all the advantages and disadvantages. However, it is not simply a question of the longest list, which determines the outcome. Because I am 'like a balance at equilibrium, without leaning to either side' (#179) it is a more a question of weighing up the pros and cons. For example it may be far more important that I live near my ageing parents than near my favourite football team.

Z: That's good. I prefer to live further south than near to Bolton.

The second way in this third method of discernment uses the imagination. The person making the choice has to imagine telling a person they have never known what they have chosen for the greater glory of God. Or the person has to imagine they are on their deathbed. Would they still have made the same choice? Finally they have to imagine they are standing before their judge on the last day and again reflect on the decision they would have wished to have made. (#185-187) As with the first way, there has to be confirmation in the form of a feeling of consolation.

It is important to notice that all three methods of discernment not only necessitate a process of confirmation but they take place within a context of prayer. Prayer is actually part of the decision-making process

There are choices for all of us. What future would we like to have? What kind of world would we like our children and grandchildren to grow up in? Ever since photographs of planet earth have been taken from space there is a feeling that the world is very fragile and needs to be cared for. How am I caring for it? Do I need to change my life style? Whatever choices we make, it is encouraging to note that decisions can take you out of God's will but never out of his reach. (2 Tim 2:13)

Z: This is all about making individual decisions but what about people in a group who have to make a decision? What happens then?

Just before we come on to that, there is a word of caution I want to inject. There can often be the feeling that we must make the right decision. Christians want to do what God wants them to do. Sometimes we can all get it wrong no matter how careful we are.

Z: Welcome to the human race.

Thankfully we are not asked to be perfect. Perfection is a very hard task master from which there is no escape. The great thing is that we do not become whole people by being perfect but by experiencing the love that holds us even when we make a mistake.

## community discernment

One could argue that community or group discernment is not as important as individual discernment. That is true up to a point but as we shall see in chapter eleven community is essential to the Christian faith.

Z: It would be difficult to conceive of a circus with only one act. Even watching clowns all the time would get tiresome and they would lose their appeal.

Church meetings are no exception in dealing with the wide range of choices that have become available. Shall we raise a large amount of money to renovate the church or shall we knock it down and build something more suitable for this day and age? What kind of building does God require of us? Does God require us to have a building at all? How much money can we raise? Could our money be more wisely used? Can we do more good by helping to alleviate world poverty or supporting a community project? Is this the time for more ecumenical cooperation? Are we being asked to stay as we are or is God calling us out into an unknown future?

A Church meeting typically begins with a time of worship and prayer. This may take a variety of forms but usually only lasts for a tiny fraction of the time the meeting will take. More often than not, the person praying will ask that those attending may be 'open to the promptings of the Spirit' as they seek to do 'the will of God'. The meeting then proceeds through a set series of agenda items, which are quite straightforward, but there is often something quite contentious to discuss along the way. I have attended many meetings that have discussed the time of Sunday morning worship and it soon becomes apparent that people turn up with their own agendas. For true discernment to take place 'it is essential that participants be willing to move away from preconceived ideas and personal preference'. (12)

Z: Does it really make any difference if a service starts at 10.30 am or 11 am?

It does to some people. In a typical discussion arguments are put forward and refuted and sometimes the debate can become quite heated depending on the protagonists and what is at stake. More often than not proceedings will draw to a conclusion with somebody proposing a motion. The Chair of the meeting will ask for a seconder and the proposition is put the vote. This is one way of conducting the business but can it really be said that a process of discernment has taken place? Is it any different to a process of decision-making, albeit in a Christian context? The matter under discussion could be major policy for the local church. This is not about a relatively unimportant issue like the colour of the paint in the church toilets but about where God is calling us, as a church, to be. The key question in discernment must always be, what is God asking of us? It is almost impossible to discover this when people come to meetings with their own pet ideas and prejudices and are therefore closed off to the 'promptings of the Spirit'. They are far removed from the notion of being indifferent. Furthermore, the atmosphere can be soured by the fact than when a vote is taken there are, inevitably, not only winners, but also losers, unless the result was unanimous but even then it is highly likely that group pressures have caused some people to put up their hands with the majority rather than be seen publicly to be in a minority. Moreover, 'sometimes those who exert the most pressure are the ones who prevail. The people on the losing side may feel ignored, beaten alienated. The feelings and contributions of minorities are often discounted and soon forgotten by those who carry the day'. (13)

Z: I know that feeling well, being on the losing side and having to pick yourself up, dust yourself down, and get on with life.

A possible way out is offered in a book called 'Grounded in God' which, not surprisingly, is written by three people in 'prayerful community'. Of course a case is made out for a sound rational approach to any community problem but discernment is not simply wrestling with issues, 'it is **not** problem solving. The goal of our discernment efforts is to find the mind of Christ'. (14) Thus, discernment becomes a central focus in any decision-making process and it is more than just, what can be the tokenism, of saying prayers before a meeting begins. 'It is a mode of prayer that involves opening our entire selves to the working of the Holy Spirit. It bids us to let go of preconceived ideas so that we can be open to new possibilities with a readiness to view things from new perspectives. Discernment beckons us to be still and listen with the ear of our heart. It draws us into alignment with God.' (15)

The presupposition for such a community is that God is actively present and that the people attending genuinely want to approach any issue with an open heart and mind. It is only under such circumstances that God is allowed into the proceedings. 'When those present centre in God and listen deeply, their varying needs and divergent views can move from discord to concord. Rather than entering into a context with factions singing competing tunes, the group as a whole can discover a true harmony, satisfying all.' (16)

Z: But what if you can't sing?

It can be seen that any discussion does not become an excuse to persuade others to one particular point of view and certainly not a way of persuading God to follow a particular course of action. Rather, it is a genuine attempt to seek God's guidance through listening to each other. This kind of listening not only involves our ears but also our eyes and our feelings. (17)

It is as though God acts as an internet service provider. Until I connect with my ISP through my own computer I am unaware of any e-mails I might have been sent and I cannot log on to the vast range of information available though the internet. The problem is that sometimes we are sent junk mail. How do we know that it is truly God who is 'sending' the information? In a sense we don't. There is no certainty and we are limited by our human fallibilities. Human discernment can sometimes go wrong.

Discernment is more likely to take place when there is no desire to reach a decision through an adversarial contest as in a court of law but rather that a consensual decision is reached. Quakers call this spiritual consensus a 'sense of the meeting'. The problem is that consensus does not fit into our usual time schedules. The meeting must be over by 10 o'clock and there are other agenda items to work through. As a result a decision may have been reached but this does not preclude the possibility that there may be a better one. There can also be a desire to 'get things done' and to be seen to be doing things. (18) God, however, works to a different time scale. 'Consensus unfolds over time and may not fit into a predesigned schedule.' (19) The difficulty is that although consensus can sometimes be reached very quickly whilst at other times there is a 'lengthy struggle'. It is certainly true that community discernment takes longer than individual discernment simply because there are more possibilities to be checked out. I certainly discovered when living in a community, simply because other people needed to be consulted, decisions took a lot longer.

Z: You couldn't do just what you wanted to do.

Not unless I wanted to ignore other people's feelings. That would mean being a dictator and there is no room for community building in a dictatorship. Sometimes, as a minister, I have been approached by somebody who has an idea for the church community. My instinct has been to say, 'I'll bring it up at the next church council.' If that meeting happens to be, say, six weeks down the line, and the meeting says, 'we must think about this', then the person who had the original idea begins to lose heart.

Z: They have probably forgotten what their idea was.

That may well be true. Maybe I needed, sometimes, to make a quick decision after a little thought and consultation rather than prolong the matter unnecessarily. However, with important questions it is surely desirable to let the Spirit have a hand in reaching the right decision rather than rushing through, for the sake of an agenda, a decision that may well turn out to be the wrong one. A compromise may be arrived at but this usually satisfies no one. In general, compromises are not energising and they are a convenient way for the chairperson to move onto the next agenda because a decision has been arrived at. For true discernment and for a consensus to be achieved an atmosphere of mutual respect is required and that, as we noted earlier, requires a ditching of preconceived ideas and ready made answers.

In his book about creating community, Scott Peck calls this process 'emptiness.' (20) For community to happen barriers to communication, 'feelings, assumptions, ideas, and motives', must be discarded, otherwise people have 'so filled their minds that they become as impervious as billiard balls'. (21)

This is not to say that conflict may not arise or that disagreements are swept under the carpet. Scott Peck in his book on community building writes 'in genuine community there are no sides' ,(22) Peck is at pains to point out that conflict avoidance is no way to create a community but community is 'a group that can fight gracefully'. This is something that Christians traditionally find very difficult. It is thought that it is better to be nice to someone rather than honest.

Z: I thought Christians were supposed to speak the truth in love.

Quite so, but people have difficult in disagreeing in a non confrontational way. There are ways of doing this in a kind way. 'Have you thought of….' or 'How about……' or 'I wonder what would happen if……..'

Peck writes that an attitude of avoiding conflict at all costs does not create a genuine community but 'pseudocommunity'. (23) 'What is diagnostic of pseudocommunity is the minimisation, the lack of acknowledgement, or the ignoring of individual differences.' (24) The rules of good etiquette apply. Everybody is courteous and polite to each other and the end- product is a well-functioning group but these rules 'crush individuality, intimacy, and honesty, and the longer it lasts the duller it gets'. (25)

Z: I think you have been in a few dull meetings!

That is sadly the case, even though I was often the chairman! I don't make any claim to be especially spiritual, but I am concerned that a process is engaged upon which produces the 'right' result. Sometimes I feel that God is elbowed out when people gather together for a church meeting. God is the very person people seem afraid to consult.

Z: You mean it's as though there is an elephant in the room and everybody is afraid to point it out?

Exactly. I have discovered that when a period of prayer or silent reflection is introduced the mood of a meeting changes. Anyone involved in counselling or spiritual direction will know it is precisely the silences that are most productive. When the words have ceased, there is room for God to have a say. In a weekend away with some young adults there was a heated discussion about the nature of community. We terminated this with half an hour of complete silence. The nature of the discussion afterwards was on a different plane altogether. Of course, it is not always practical to have a long period of silence during a 'business' meeting but it is perfectly possible to place a time of prayer or reflection in the middle of the agenda and that has the effect of placing the meeting in a different context. If nothing else, it is a reminder that we are trying to wait upon God in our work. I was recently at a district synod where the whole day took place in the context of the Methodist covenant service. This was very productive and creative because again the process focussed minds in the right place.

'Something happens to us when we consult one another in Christian community.' (26) Insights emerge which as individuals we would simply not have thought about. Many times I have gone to a meeting with an idea.

Z: Which no doubt you thought was the right one and the only one!

That's true, but as a result of truly listening to each other a much better idea emerged. When we think we are right there is no possibility of discovery and no possibility of dialogue. If I know I have the truth what point is there in listening to anybody else?

'Because God often reveals part of the picture to one person and another part to another person, it is prudent to consult one another to discern God's counsel, guidance, and direction, even if there is no apparent reason to do so.' (27) The process of community consultation is also a good protection against arrogance – the feeling that I, and only I, have heard from God, and only I therefore have to be listened to.

Z: May the saints preserve you from being always right!

The problem is that to truly listen to another demands a high level of concentration. More often than not we are already forming in our minds a response, even a put down, to the speaker rather than truly listening and honouring what has been said. One reason for the difficulty is that as a result of listening we may need to change our ideas and that would seemingly put us in a position of weakness. Bonhoeffer has some challenging words to say on the subject of listening. 'He who can no longer listen to his brother will soon be no longer listening to God either; he will be doing nothing but prattle in the presence of God too. This is the beginning of the death of the spiritual life, and in the end there is nothing left but spiritual chatter and clerical condescension arrayed in pious words.' (28)

Z: What a phrase, prattling in the presence of God.

Perhaps that is why many people find committees so boring, they have become simply a matter of charging through a long agenda and listening to reports of events that happened long ago. I have often found it strange to go to an annual general meeting and listen to minutes of a meeting which took place twelve months previously and which, in themselves, recorded events which had taken place in the previous twelve months. In others words we were listening to a record of events that many have happened nearly two years previously!!

Z: Life is just too short. No wonder people lose the will to live or simply lose the desire to sit on committees.

I have said before that God is in the present, nowhere else. The present moment is all that we have and the task is to discern the mind of Christ in the present. This entails not just left brain activity but also right brain because we have to get in touch with our feelings and our creative impulses. No longer are we trying to solve a problem and move on to the next agenda item but genuinely seeking to discern where God wants us to be. As with individual discernment when the decision reached is truly of God the result is energising and life giving. I have sometimes returned home after a church meeting as though I had an elephant in each pocket and not in the least bit energised.

Z: The people must have thought you had a lot of trunk calls to make.

The evening, or a particular decision, had not been life giving, quite the reverse. Spiritual discernment, genuine prayerful listening to each other, a desire to discover what the next step is that God wants us to take, and achieving this through consensus offers a different route.

Z: Does it involve anything more than just listening to each other?

Something quite basic is to arrange for people to sit in a circle. This enables people to see each other and to listen with their eyes as well as their ears. A circle also suggests equality.

Z: Just like King Arthur and his knights of the round table.

Quite so. It also helps to have comfortable seats, and a lit candle as a reminder of Christ's presence.

Z: Even I might like that kind of meeting. Any there any more guidelines?

I have already said attentive listening. That means not interrupting and not formulating what you want to say whilst someone else is speaking. Incidentally, you are always interrupting.

Z: I'm very good at it.

Indeed, but it can be very irritating. Most of the time we interrupt because we want to say more although it may be important to interrupt if the person is straying from the subject or just talking too much.

Z: Yes, there are those who need more time to gather their thoughts and can do it better in quietness.

For that reason it is helpful to pause between speakers to absorb what has been said. Another suggestion is to speak only on behalf of yourself and, moreover, not challenge what others have to say. Finally, sit lightly to your own desires and opinions.

Z: That last point is a surprise.

The reason is that no one person can grasp the mind of God. It is therefore vital always to be open to the possibility that God can change our minds, or at the very least, refine our convictions. The end product is often surprising. God has a wonderful capacity to break through our preconceptions and take us in unexpected directions. Of course, God does not show us the whole picture all at once. Discernment is about the next step not the whole journey.

Our next step is to discover the direction the church is going in but before that we need to make some general points about the church and the community.

## Points to Ponder:

1. How would you describe your experience of group decision making?

2. How do you feel about any decisions you disagreed with?

3. How easy do you find it to disagree with people in public?

4. Is it more important to be honest or to keep quiet?

5. Why is it difficult to be a Christian and not belong to a community?

# Meditation

Spend some time going over the events of your day. Which were the deadening experiences? Which were the energising experiences? How did you feel about the day? Where was God absent or present?

# References

1. Farnham, Suzanne G .,Gill, Joseph P. ,McLean, R. Taylor and Ward, Susan M.. Listening Hearts, Morehouse , 2002. p.32.
2. Alfonso, Herbert, The Personal Vocation, Centrum Ignatianum Spiritualitatis, 1993, p.28
3. Farnham et al, op. cit., p.33
4. # indicates the appropriate paragraph in Puhl, Louis J., The Spiritual Exercises of Ignatius Loyola, Loyola University Press, 1951: ## indicates the appropriate paragraph in Ganss, George E. Spiritual Exercises, Paulist, 1991.
5. Puhl, p.12
6. The Methodist covenant service was instigated by John Wesley but it is not easy to say whether he had any knowledge of Ignatius. In fact Sheldrake asserts "I have not found any evidence of the assertion" that "Wesley knew of the Spiritual Exercises and was familiar with imaginative scripture prayer". See The Way Supplement, Ignatian Spirituality in Ecumenical Context, Summer 1990, Number 68.
7. De Mello, Anthony, Awareness, Fount, 1990, p.134
8. ibid., p.118

9. Valles, Carlos, <u>Mastering Sadhana,</u> Fount, 1991, p.53

10. Lonsdale, David, <u>Eyes To See, Ears to Hear</u>, DLT., 1990, p 71.

11. ibid.

12. Farnham Suzanne G., Hull, Stephanie A., McLean R. Taylor, <u>Grounded in God</u>, Morehouse, 1999, p.33

13. ibid., p.31

14. ibid., p.7

15. ibid.

16. ibid., p.8

17. see, for example, Gans, George E., <u>Ignatius of Loyola</u>, Paulist, 1991, p.151

18. The desire to solve a problem and actually do something is particularly a male problem. See Gray,John, <u>Men are from Mars, Women are from Venus,</u> Thorsons, 1993. Especially chapter 2. Note also that at the top of the Mount of Transfiguration the disciples wanted to do something. Matt. 17 ff

19. Farnham et al, 1999 op. cit., p.32

20. Peck, Scott, <u>The Different Drum</u>, Arrow, 1990. p.94ff

21. ibid., p.95

22. ibid, p.71

23. ibid., p.86ff

24. ibid,. p.88

25. ibid., p.89

26. Farnham, 2002, op. cit., p.54

27. ibid., p.55

28. Bonhoeffer, <u>Life Together</u> op. cit., p.75

# Chapter 10

## WHATEVER HAPPENED TO COMMUNITY?

A few years ago, I was sitting in my London suburban manse when a funeral cortege drew up in front of the house across the road. There was nothing unusual about this neighbourhood in that it was a typical road in a typical London borough. I was on speaking terms with some people and a nodding acquaintance with others. However, it came as a shock to realise that the man across the road had died and I knew nothing about this until the hearse pulled up outside. It occurred to me that if I hadn't happened to be at home at that particular moment I might never have found out about his death.

Z: So much for community!

This is a far cry from the street where I lived as a boy in a Manchester suburb. I regularly 'played out' with my friends in the road and it seemed to me then that we knew by name everybody in the road and my parents would have known immediately had someone died. Indeed all the curtains in neighbouring windows would have been drawn. It would have been unthinkable that a major family crisis could have taken place and other people, apart from the immediate family, not known about it. This was not because people lived in each other's pockets but because there was a feeling of community. People were genuinely concerned about each other.

Z: Oh dear, this sounds like a nostalgic stroll down memory lane.

During my childhood, very little happened on a Sunday. Shops were shut and there was no sport and so church was one of the few places where people could meet. They tended to be the centre of local communities, genuine meeting places and centres of entertainment. Historically churches were built and communities built around them. The church building was the centre to which all gravitated. It is quite symbolic that many of these churches, because of road building schemes, new estates and so on, are now on the margins of their community.

Apart from my family, the church was where I felt I belonged. Not only were there the usual services of worship on Sundays but also there was the weekly youth club, the Sunday night fellowship and other social activities where one met friends and acquaintances.

Z: And girl friends no doubt. Never mind, your wild oats have now been turned into prunes and muesli.

Every Easter Monday we went on a ramble in the Peak District and every Christmas Eve we went round the houses of church members singing carols into the small hours of Christmas Day. On New Year's Eve there was a major church social to dance in the New Year.

Z: Sounds like a real rave up - you dancing the waltz and foxtrot.

You would be surprised what I got up to but I agree with you. It is easy to look back and be filled with nostalgia for what were supposedly the 'good old days'. People say that during the two world wars of the last century a community spirit was engendered that has not pertained before or since. However, it would be dangerous to idealise the past, as though life was idyllic. Without doubt, life was not all good in the past and certainly, in a small village, life could be very claustrophobic. People longed to escape to the city, where there was anonymity and freedom. Suffice it to say that there is now much more a feeling of 'doing your own thing'; of being independent for as long as possible. Indeed, it is counted as a measure of success if you can be independent.

Z: Who needs other people? Just about every act in a circus!

You have 'arrived' if you can manage out of your own resources without recourse to any outside help. This begs the question that we are all acutely and intimately dependent on each other. Society runs on a tight mesh of interdependency. To be totally self-sufficient and live the ultimate 'good life' would mean, apart from anything else, having one's own power supply as well as fresh water.

In addition to all this, we live in boxes, spend a lot of time looking at boxes, be they computers or television screens, and travel around in boxes on wheels, safely insulated and separated from each other. (1) We drive from our home to our destination often with no contact with other people. The corner shop has disappeared almost without trace, the local post office is following suit, as is the local pub. The result of this style of living has been that many people lead very lonely lives. During my ministry, I have all too frequently met elderly people who spend many, many hours, sometimes days, on their own. The visits from 'meals on wheels' and possibly a care worker punctuate the monotony of their day. The television is usually switched on in the corner to give the feeling that there is somebody else around. However, this escape from loneliness just adds to the tedium of the day.

Z: I wonder what people did before television invaded our homes? Did they actually talk to each other? Did they actually have more time?

The organization Help the Aged say that over a million people feel lonely and isolated. Many have little family. Most have hardly any friends. Some just get the occasional visit from a carer. Nearly five million older people (that's half of the over 65s) depend mainly on their television for company. Over one million say they feel trapped in their own homes. Is it surprising that many are so depressed they withdraw from society? I can think of an elderly gentleman who lived alone but was frequently seen walking the streets of the town at night just to see other human faces.

Nor is it just old people who are lonely. I can recall the mother who had just given birth to her baby and was confined to the house because she was not allowed to drive. After three weeks, she was beginning to despair. There was the hospital patient who no one ever visited and the woman who had an abortion 30 years ago and who has never been able to tell anyone about it. There was the loneliness of the university student away from home for the first time; the man going through a heart breaking divorce and nobody asked about him because the concern was more for his partner and children; the lady crippled with arthritis and no longer able to do the things that she once did and there was the pastor who was so much 'in role' that she was not able to develop any long lasting friendships. The list of lonely people is endless. Scott Peck writes, 'trapped in our tradition of rugged individualism, we are an extraordinarily lonely people. So lonely, in fact, that many cannot even acknowledge their loneliness to themselves, much less to others'. (2) He talks of the need for a 'soft individualism', which recognises that we cannot be truly ourselves until we recognise our lack of wholeness and self-sufficiency. Peck writes that 'we must recognise that we live in a time in which our need for community has itself become critical'. (3)

From a psychological point of view,

Z: You said no long words.

Just let me continue....the worst kind of punishment or torture an individual can undergo is solitary confinement and sensory deprivation. Experiments have been carried out in which individuals are placed in an environment which has as little stimulation as possible. The individual is blindfolded, ear plugged and suspended in a tank of water maintained at body temperature. This treatment quickly leads to disorientation and hallucinations of various kinds. It has long been known, by those who wish to torture others, that placing someone in solitary isolation can quickly lead to a breakdown of resistance. In this respect therefore people can clearly be seen as social animals. This is also true of creatures lower down the evolutionary scale. One has only to study the behaviour of bees or ants or flocks of birds. They offer no room for individualism.

From a theological point of view,

Z: Another long word.

...the roots of individualism can be traced back to Harnack. He is a representative of a broad tendency of liberal theology at the end of the 19<sup>th</sup> century and the beginning of the 20<sup>th</sup>. He put forward the idea that the reign of God could come only to each individual. Thus, the Sermon on the Mount is merely about the right intentions of each individual and the Church is a union of individuals who are saved as individuals through their faith in the gospel. However, we shall see in the next chapter that a much more important strand in the Old Testament is the concept of the nation of Israel and developing out of this in the New Testament is the community of the twelve disciples. The Gospel is certainly imparted to individuals but individuals as members of a group. One could argue that from the beginning of humankind, God saw the need for people to exist in relationship to each other and not in isolation. 'Then the Lord God said, "it is not good that the man should be alone; I will make him a helper as his partner".' (Gen. 2:18) The Greeks had a similar view. Aristotle wrote, 'man is by nature a social animal; an individual who is unsocial naturally and not accidentally is either beneath our notice or more than human. Society is something in nature that precedes the individual. Anyone who either cannot lead the common life or is so self-sufficient as not to need to, and therefore does not partake of society is either a beast or a god'. (4) 'We were born to live together,' wrote Seneca, 'our society is an arch of stones joined together, which would break down if each did not support the other.' (5)

Z: That sounds pretty obvious.

It may sound obvious. Strands of thread bound together are much stronger than a single thread. Nevertheless, there has been a strong drive towards independence and individualism the origins of which go back to the beginnings of the Enlightenment. The movement reached its peak during the time of Margaret Thatcher's premiership. This was the era of 'get on your bike' and do your own thing. It was the age of privatisation with the accompanying danger of privatising God; religion could become simply an issue between me and my maker and the corporate nature of Christianity was ignored. We are still reaping the harvest of this philosophy today with the increased cynicism about organised religion and the desire for people to seek their own salvation. They feed their spirituality by going for a walk, digging the garden or carving some wood in the shed rather than in church on a Sunday. Mrs. Thatcher obviously had never heard the warning issued to people about not going to the funeral of their own independence. Etzioni, although writing from an American perspective says 'the eighties was a decade in which "I" was writ large, in which the celebration of the self became a virtue…Now is the time to push back the pendulum. The times call for an age of reconstruction, in which we put a new emphasis on "we," on values we share, on the spirit of community'. (6) 'Our society is suffering from a severe case of deficient we-ness and the values only communities can properly uphold; restoring communities and their moral voice is what our current conditions require'. (7) Scott Peck in his book about the creation of true community goes even further, 'in and through community lies the salvation of the world'. (8)

The theologian Tillich writes 'only in the continuous encounter with other persons does the person become and remain a person. The place of this encounter is the community'. (9) This is corroborated by Buber, the Jewish philosopher, who says, 'all real living is meeting'. (10) For Buber, this real meeting takes place within an 'I-Thou' relationship. There are two worlds, an impersonal world and a personal one. Between these two worlds, there is a frontier that is difficult to cross. Buber himself uses the example of a tree which remains an 'it', an object, a thing which I can examine from the outside, unless I have the capacity to enter into personal communion with it in which case the tree becomes a 'thou'. Much of the time people relate to each other in very superficial ways, even when they have known each other for a long time.

I grew up in a family full of love and security, but where my parents never talked with friends about politics or religion because it was thought that such a conversation might rock the boat and destroy the friendship. Confrontation had to be avoided at all costs even perhaps at the cost of honesty. The same often applies today. Some people are happy to talk about the weather, or sport, or last night's episode of the television soap, but not about anything of consequence and certainly not about their feelings. One could argue that with the current explosion of new ways of communicating with each other the situation is getting worse. There is a preference for sound bites and text messaging and it is becoming increasingly difficult to communicate with each other at a meaningful level. Twittering is now the order of the day.

Z: Even I can see that our new ways of connecting with each other could also be the very same ways which lead to greater isolation although there might be some exceptions. I happen to know that some of your grandchildren and other family members keep in touch with each other through Facebook. These new ways of communicating can have their benefits.

They certainly do. For example, Avaaz is a global campaign network which uses the web to ensure that the values and views of the world's people inform global decision-making. At present, there are over 5 million members and issues such as climate change, peace and human rights in the Middle East and Burma, protecting forests and oceans, as well as organized crime and the horrific rape trade have all been highlighted and influence brought to bear on the decision makers.

However, to come back to my original point, by its very nature I think Facebook lends itself only to superficial contact. The Buddhist monk Thich Nhat Hanh writes about a deep malaise in society. 'We can send e-mail and faxes anywhere in the world, we have pagers and cellular telephones, and yet in our families and neighbourhoods we do not speak to each other. There is a kind of vacuum inside us, and we attempt to fill it by eating, reading, talking, smoking, drinking, watching TV, going to movies, and even overworking. We absorb so much violence and insecurity every day that we are like time bombs ready to explode.' (13)

We pass as ships in the night without ever really making contact. Yet as Scott Peck points out 'the principles of good communication are the basic principles of community-building'. (14) The words 'communicate' and 'community' come from the same root, the Latin word for common. 'Never in the history of communication have we had so many means of communication, yet we remain islands. There is little real communication between the members of one family, between the individuals in society, and between nations. We have not cultivated the arts of listening and speaking. We have to learn ways to communicate again.' (15)

Z: As you have said before, perhaps we have to listen before we can speak.

John Powell explains that there are five levels of communication which people engage in at one time or another. (6) The fifth level represents the least willingness to communicate ourselves to others whilst the successive descending levels indicate an increasingly intimate communication. Level five is that of the cliché conversation. This is where there is polite conversation at the party or where someone is passed in the street and there is the enquiry 'how are you?' without any expectation of a detailed health report, merely the answer 'I'm fine'. Or there is a general statement about the weather but nothing else.

Level four is reached when the facts about others are reported. The conversation has no emotional content. There is no revealing of feelings and so almost nothing about our self is given away. We are simply telling others what so-and –so has said or done. Ideas and judgments come in at level three. Here there is some communication of myself as a person because I am telling others about my thoughts, ideas, opinions and decisions. This may take a certain amount of courage and I may return to a previous level if I am not encouraged by your comments.

Z: I hope you are encouraged by <u>my</u> comments.

I certainly am. They usually make me think a bit more. Anyway let me continue with level two which is labelled by Powell as the 'gut' level. Communication is much more than the sharing of ideas. It is also a sharing of my feelings, my emotions. In other words we can share with each other not just at the head level, in the realm of ideas, but at the gut level, in the realm of feelings. One of the secrets of being an integrated and whole person is when we can get our head and our heart together. A few years ago I applied for a job because my head was telling me that this was the thing to do. This is what was expected. However, my gut feelings, if I had but listened to them, were telling me something quite different. The result was that my interview was a disaster and I wasn't offered the job. It is my feelings that are peculiar to me. The worst possible thing that can be said to anybody is 'I know how you feel'. However well meant that phrase is, no one can know how someone else is feeling because they have a different life experience. How can they know how someone feels without asking them? We might empathise with someone at the loss of his or her spouse and convey our sadness but it might be very presumptuous to say 'I know how you feel'. The bereaved person may actually be glad that their beloved has departed this life! We cannot assume how the other person is feeling.

Z: As the old joke has it that would make an ASS of U and ME.

The only way we can know how someone is feeling is when he or she has the courage to tell us. This is level two. Level one is 'peak' communication. "All deep and authentic friendships, and especially the union of those who are married, must be based on absolute openness and honesty". (17) There is no suggestion that this is easy to attain but there are moments in our encounters when two people can feel 'an almost perfect and mutual empathy'. (18) Powell gives the illustration of two musical instruments playing exactly the same note, filled with and giving forth precisely the same sound. This is peak communication.

There is a price to pay for emotional honesty. We might not be taken seriously, or listened to or, in our vulnerability; we might be abused in one way or another. Consequently we sometimes prefer to be dishonest and we defend our dishonesty 'on the grounds that it might hurt others; and, having rationalised our phoniness into nobility, we settle for superficial relationships'. (19)

However, just occasionally, the frontier is crossed and the other person becomes a 'thou', a deeper relationship has been forged. This is the beginning of community. It is this kind of community which Scott Peck has written about and seeks to develop in his workshops. There is in fact, a network of people who have been to these workshops called 'community building in Britain', the very existence of which suggests a strong need in people for community.

The assumption in this scheme of things is that level one is the place to aim for. When we have achieved intimacy then we have arrived and all will be well. This is currently thought to be the objective in many churches which have a 'small group' way of working and it is ultimately assumed that being intimate with God will bring the believer into a wonderful state of grace. These views are challenged by Myers in a very helpful book called 'The search to belong'. (20)

Myers builds on the work of Edward T. Hall who identified four spaces in human interaction, namely public, social, personal, and intimate. Depending on the kind of space we are in, we stand at a distance from each other ranging from twelve or more feet to eighteen inches or actually touching.

Myers relates these same four categories to community, or a sense of belonging. 'How we occupy physical space....tells others whether we want them to belong'. (21) The important point is that 'for harmony and for the sake of health, we need significant belonging in all four spaces; public, social, personal, and intimate'. (22) In other words there is no drive to arrive at the intimate. Each category is significant in its own right and in daily life the healthy person moves freely between all four categories.

Public space occurs when people are brought together through an outside influence. This could be a congregation at worship, a concert audience, fans at a football match, or travellers on an aeroplane. In the latter case, although the physical distance for adjacent passengers is intimate, the space is actually public unless conversation takes place which leads to another level. Relationships in public space can be very significant and certainly engender a sense of belonging.

In social space 'we provide information that helps others decide whether they connect with us. We get just enough information to decide to keep this person in this space or move them to another space'. (23) In this space first impressions can be very important as we decide whether to share any of our life's experiences with other people and wonder whether they could be part of our personal space. Such spaces may be a youth club, a work environment or talking to the neighbour over the garden fence.

When friends become 'close' friends they are in personal space. We are able to share personal and private thoughts and feelings with them. These people know more about us than a casual acquaintance. However, it is in intimate space that we share 'naked' experiences. In actual fact we have very few relationships that are intimate, 'these people know the 'naked truth' about us and we are not ashamed'. (24)

Z: Naked!! This is getting very interesting!

Trust you to get the wrong end of the stick. When talking about community, Myers specifies a symbol. Just as water has the chemical symbol $H_2O$ so community has the symbol $Pu_8S_4P_2I$.

Z: This is getting harder!

This is simply a formula and a convenient way of saying that for every one part of significant intimate belonging, there are two parts personal, four parts social, and eight parts public. If this community compound is altered then healthy community may not exist. In other words, to concentrate simply on small intimate groups as a way of building up a church may not be the best way forward. All parts of the formula have to be present for a healthy community.

Myers is at pains to point out that 'intimate' is 'not the most important, the most real, or the most authentic relationship. (25) For Myers all connections are significant and it is all four spaces 'where we connect, grow roots, and satisfy our search for community'. (26) This is his point of departure from Peck and Powell. There is authenticity in whatever space you are in.

Z: Well that's a relief. I can feel authentic where ever I am.

Yep. Precisely there, where you are, you find your connections and sense of belonging. Of course, this sense of community has, for a Christian, roots in the bible.

*Malcolm Rothwell*

You might like to skip the next chapter, Zeno, because it gets a bit technical and there are quotes from all sorts of learned people.

Z: Not me. I'll try and keep up.

## **Points to Ponder:**

1. Consider your own life in the light of Myer's formula $Pu_8S_4P_2I$. Try to name for yourself 8 public spaces, 4 social spaces, 2 personal spaces and 1 intimate space in which you belong. Are there any elements missing from your life?

2. Consider the life of a community to which you belong. E.g. a church or a work place. Repeat the exercise in question 1.

3. How well do you know your neighbours?

4. What kind of things could you do to promote a healthier community where you live?

5. Has community life improved or declined during your life time? What are the reasons for your answer?

## **Meditation:**

O God, the source of our common life,
when we are dry and scattered,
when we are divided and alone,
we long for connection, we long for community
**Breath of God, breathe on us.**

With those we live beside,
who are often strange to us,
whom we may be afraid to approach,
yet who have riches of friendship to share,
we long for connection, we long for community.
**Breath of God, breathe on us.**

With those we have only heard of,
who see with different eyes,
whose struggles we try to imagine,
whose fierce joy we wish we could grasp,
we long for connection, we long for community.
**Breath of God, breathe on us.**

With those we shall never know,
but whose lives are linked with ours,
whose shared ground we stand on,
and whose common air we breathe,
we long for connection, we long for community.
**Breath of God, breathe on us.**

When we are dry and scattered,
when we are divided and alone,
when we are cut off from the source of our life,
open our graves, O God,
that all your people
may be free to breathe, strong to move,
and joyful to stand together
to celebrate your name. **Amen** (27)

# **References**

1. It is interesting to note that a common expectation of people staying in hotels is that they will be 'en suite'. Indeed a mark of having 'arrived' is to have an en suite bedroom in your house. This is a far cry from years ago when many people would be expected to use the same toilet facilities.

2. Peck, Scott, The different drum, Arrow books 1988, p.58

3. ibid., p.80

4. Aronson, Elliott, The social animal, W.H. Freeman and Company 1980, p. xvii

5. Kirkpatrick, Frank G., The ethics of community, Blackwell 2001, p.62

6. Amitai, Etzioni, The spirit of community, Touchstone 1993, p.25

7. ibid., p.26

8. Tillich, Paul, The courage to be, Fontana 1971, p. 93

9. Buber, Martin, I and Thou, T & T Clark, Edinburgh 1984, p11

10. MacMurray, John, Persons in relation, Faber and Faber 1961, p.12

11. ibid., p.17

12. Hanh, Thich Nhat, Living Buddha, Living Christ, Riverhead Books, 1995, p.87

13. Peck, op. cit., p.83

14. Hanh, op. cit., p. 102

15. Powell, John, Why am I afraid to tell you who I am? Fontana, Collins 1975, p. 54ff

16. ibid., p.61

17. ibid., p.62

18. ibid. p.88
19. Myers, Joseph R. <u>The Search to Belong;
    Rethinking Intimacy, Community and Small
    Groups,</u> Zondervan, 2003
20. ibid., p. 36
21. ibid., p. 41
22. ibid., p.143
23. ibid.
24. ibid,. p.63
25. ibid.
26. ibid.
27. Morley, Janet, (Ed.), <u>Bread of Tomorrow</u>, SPCK.
    Christian Aid, 1992, p.148

# Chapter 11

## BIBLICAL ROOTS OF COMMUNITY

Z: I want you to tell me in words of one syllable where you get this idea from that community is important for Christians.

If you really want to know and you are not pulling my leg I'll try and explain it to you although words of one syllable might stretch me a bit.

Z: Listen, if I was pulling your leg you would know about it. For once in my life I am trying to be serious, now get on with it.

Well, I think you probably know that in all four gospels the ministry of Jesus is preceded by that of John the Baptist who preaches to the Israelites that God will create for Abraham a new Israel, a new community, from the stones of the desert. (Luke 3:8). A biblical scholar called Lohfink argues that 'the Baptist chose the *desert* as the site of his preaching so that the people had to *go out* to him, is properly understood only against the background of Israel's Exodus tradition.' (1) In other words the important thing for John is the establishment of community, a community that began with the family of Abraham and then developed into a clan, a group and, eventually, a people, the people of Israel.

Z: Yes, I have heard all that stuff about the people of Israel but that is about the Jewish faith. What about Christianity?

The question is really about whether the establishment of a community only relates to Jewish people or is it for non-Jews, that is, Gentiles as well. Lohfink writes that 'Jesus in no way excluded the Gentiles from salvation but he himself directed his attention to Israel.'(2) In defending this case he uses such texts as Matt 15:24 where Jesus says 'I was sent only to the lost sheep of the house of Israel' and Mark 7:27 'let the children be fed first, for it is not fair to take the children's food and throw it to the dogs.'

Z: By 'dogs' presumably Jesus had Gentiles in mind.

Exactly. Lohfink further argues that Jesus' encounters with the Gentiles were sporadic and not deliberately sought. Indeed, Jesus is astonished when he finds faith in the Gentile centurion. (Matt8: 5-10) However, there are also many examples where Jesus ministers to Gentiles and to say that he is mainly concerned with 'the gathering and restoration of the people of God – the gathering of Israel' seems to contradict the evidence of the gospels. Jesus' thinking is certainly related to Israel but it is not limited to Israel.

Z: Please get on with it. This is getting boring.

However, Lohfink concludes that 'even when Israel as a whole refused his message, he did not abandon the idea of community, the idea that the reign of God must have a people; instead he concentrated on his circle of disciples.

219

(3) 'Do not be afraid little flock, for it is your Father's good pleasure to give you the kingdom.' (Luke 12:32) 'You are those who have stood by me in my trials; and I confer on you, just as my Father has conferred on me, a kingdom, so that you may eat and drink at my table in my kingdom, and you will sit on thrones judging the twelve tribes of Israel.' (Luke 22: 28–30)

Z: Aha. So this is where the twelve disciples come in. Why didn't he choose eleven or thirteen? Was Jesus superstitious?

John the Baptist was considered very important by Jesus (see Mark 11:30, Matt 11:11, Luke 7:28) and shortly after his preaching Jesus chose twelve disciples. In fact, this is almost the first thing that he did in his ministry. It is not difficult to see the significance of this number. The twelve tribes of Israel no longer existed but 'the complete restoration of the twelve-tribe people was expected for the eschatological time of salvation'. (4) In other words this deliberate choice of Jesus was a 'symbolic prophetic action' (5) pointing forward to the expected time when Israel as a nation would be restored.

Z: I see. The number twelve is highly significant. Even I can understand that!

There is some confirmation for the supposition that the first disciples of Jesus were known as 'the Twelve' before they became known as apostles. Matthew mentions only 'the twelve' (6:30) and this usage is in line with previous conceptions for the occasion is the return of the Twelve from the mission on which they had been sent as envoys. (6:7-13) Mark uses 'the Twelve' terminology like Matthew, except that Matthew never uses the title 'Twelve' without also adding 'disciples'. Luke, in contrast, apart from the passages in which he is dependent on Mark, has the simple 'Twelve' only twice (8:1, 9:12). Indeed, early on in his account, Luke declares his specific apostolic interest, 'He called His disciples to Him, and from among them, He chose twelve and named them Apostles' (6:13). Having so named them, Luke uses the same title on three other occasions. (17:5, 22:14, 24: 10). On the basis of this evidence, Reid comes to the conclusion that 'the Twelve' or the 'twelve disciples' is a more original title than the term Apostles. 'The title of apostle may represent a later emphasis on the apostolic office'. (6) Campenhausen agrees with this conclusion. 'It is in fact true that 'the Twelve' are the oldest and most venerable group within the primitive community, but it was precisely as 'the Twelve' and originally hardly at all as apostles, that they enjoyed their corporate status. It was only at a later stage that they were first made into apostles.'(7)

Z: I think you have made your point that the Twelve were very important.

Yes. It seems that Jesus held the Twelve in a special kind of relationship and this is implied in the text previously mentioned, that they would sit upon the twelve thrones to judge the twelve tribes of Israel. This reference also implies that in Jesus' mind there is a relation between His Twelve and the twelve sons of Jacob from where the tribes of Israel get their names. Jesus knew himself to be setting up a new covenant with God that would supersede the old covenant of Moses. The new Twelve is the way that the new Israel would make its start just as the old Israel emanated from the twelve sons of Jacob. It does seem, therefore, that the Twelve had an official status right from the start.

This conclusion is supported by the fact that in the Acts of the Apostles there is the account of the steps taken to fill up the vacancy in the Twelve created by the betrayal of Judas. (Acts 1:15-26) However in the account of James, the son of Zebedee, being put to death by Herod Agrippa I, no attempt was made to fill the vacancy. The implication of this is that in so far as the Twelve had a special status conferred on them by Jesus, it was a personal thing that could not be transferred or removed. It could be forfeited by misconduct, but it could not be passed on to another in the event of a death. Further evidence of this special status of the Twelve is given by the fact that although Paul claimed parity with the Twelve in the matter of Apostleship, he never claimed to be one of the Twelve.

Z: I knew that Jesus had some disciples but I never realised the importance of their number or, indeed, their status apart from being disciples.

They certainly did. It is obvious that the Twelve had an official status right from the start. If one is appointed to perform a particular task, that is simply a function, but if it becomes necessary to appoint successors over a period of time, in order that the function be continued then that function becomes an office. As stated above this is the first thing that Jesus did. He gathered the Twelve around him. In other words he gathered together a visible community. Jesus did not write a book or a creed or rule of life or system of thought but entrusted his teaching, indeed his Kingdom, to this small community of people.

Z: If these twelve were representing the twelve tribes of Israel then I suppose it is inevitable that they all had to be men.

As we know, the Twelve were exclusively male. Of course it was a male dominated, patriarchal society but that apart, if women had been chosen, the symbolism would have been lost. By definition, the twelve sons of Jacob could not be represented by women.

Z: Of course not. They were his sons!!! I'm not stupid.

As I was saying, although the Twelve did not include women, they were certainly involved in the small community Jesus gathered round himself. Jesus had women in close attendance. (Luke 8: 1-3, see also Mark 15: 40-41) They served, they followed and one of the first professions of faith was by Martha. ( John 11:27) This is often overlooked because most people tend to concentrate on Peter's confession of faith at Caeserea Philippi; 'you are the Messiah, the Son of the living God'. (Matt; 16:16) As you know, Peter became the 'rock' on which the church was built and, in effect, it's first Pope.

Z: Isn't that fascinating? I wonder what would have happened if women had written the gospels! We might have had a St. Martha's in Rome instead of St. Peter's. Perhaps the first pope would have been a woman.

I think you are getting a bit carried away. Let me bring you back on track. After his death, the continuing ministry of Jesus is entrusted to this small community of The Twelve.

Z: I'm sorry to be so ignorant and I do understand what you have already said but where does the Kingdom of God come into all this. I thought that figured a lot in the teachings of Jesus and surely Kingdom is to do with community.

Well done Zeno. You are not such a fool as I thought you were. Some sense comes not only out of the mouths of babes and youngsters but also out of the mouths of clowns. You are absolutely right. It is almost a truism to say that with the ministry of Jesus the reign of God has begun to arrive although it may be more correct to say that in Jesus' own conception, he did not bring the kingdom, it was rather the kingdom that swept him along in his wake.' (8) This rule of God does not imply the rule of humans. In other words there is no suggestion of human domination. Lohfink writes 'in a community of *brothers* no *fathers* are permitted to rule'. (9)

Z: I hope we can add sisters.

I would certainly like to add sisters but note that in some branches of Christianity, even today, there is no equality between male and female, in spite of Paul writing there is no distinction. (Gal. 3: 28)

Z: I find it very funny in a very painful kind of way that woman are sometimes denied authority or priesthood, or the possibility of becoming a bishop. I know that women have different biological equipment to men but aren't women made in the image of God as well as men?

There you go again, trying to side-track me. Let me get back to the Kingdom.

Z: If you must. Perhaps you could tell me what the essential requirement is to be a citizen of this Kingdom.

Citizenship of the Kingdom is summed up in one word; a word that was taken from the secular world at the time of Jesus so it did not have any religious connotations. This word carried no overtones of authority, officialdom, rule, dignity, or power. It is the Greek word 'diakonia' meaning 'service'. It is precisely this word that is often translated in English by 'ministry' and its derivatives.

Z: I just knew you wouldn't be able to resist quoting some Greek. Can you be more specific please?

The essential meaning of the word is connected with waiting at table, serving food and pouring wine, a task that every Greek would regard as self-abasing. The distinction between master and servant was most apparent at the meal table and quite clearly the servant could be seen to be inferior. In the New Testament the word 'diakonia' is used in its original sense of waiting at table (Luke 17;8, John 12:2) and the word also occurs in its extended meaning of preparing meals and caring for the bodily needs of others (e.g. Luke 10:40, Acts 6:1, Matt. 4:11). Given this usage of the word, the impact of Jesus' words cannot be over estimated. 'The kings of the Gentiles lord it over them; and those in authority over them are called benefactors. But not so with you; rather the greatest among you must become like the youngest, and the leader like one who serves. For who is greater, the one who is at the table or the one who serves? Is it not the one at the table? But I am among you as one who serves.' (Luke 22: 25-27)

Z: So any idea of authority is derived from being a servant.

Exactly. Not a slave, mark you, a servant. Jesus does not ask us to be slaves because slaves have no choice. Moreover slaves are driven. Jesus invites. We have been given the freedom to choose to follow him or not to follow him.

Z: Is that all there is to it – just being a servant?

Not quite. Jesus does not restrict his use of 'diakonia' to service at table or caring for the bodily needs of others. His fundamental concern is with living for others. (Mark 9:35, 10: 43-45, Matt. 20:26-28) The spirit and manner of this 'diakonia' which Jesus gives both by precept and by example is that of a completely personal service. Moreover, a person becomes a disciple of Jesus in so far as they attempt to serve others. This is an essential element in being a citizen of God's Kingdom. There can be no suggestions of pride, greed or self-assertiveness. There can be no suggestion of power. In Mark's gospel the Twelve are arguing about who is the greatest amongst them and Jesus says 'whoever wants to be first must be last of all and servant of all'. (Mark 9:35) In the next chapter of the same gospel the sons of Zebedee are asking Jesus whether they can sit on either side of him when he comes in his glory. This request receives short shrift from Jesus (Mark 10: 35-38) who goes on to say 'you know that among the Gentiles those whom they recognise as their rulers lord it over them, and their great ones are tyrants over them. But it is not so among you; but whoever wishes to become great among you must become your servant, and whoever wishes to be first among you must be slave of all. For the Son of Man came not to be served but to serve, and to give his life a ransom for many'. (Mark 10: 42-45)

Z: So Jesus is a servant by example. But if you are right isn't it odd that there is such a hierarchy in some sections of Christianity? It must be very difficult feeling like a servant let alone acting like one if you live in a posh bishop's palace or wear sumptuous robes. Doesn't Jesus say something about the poor being blessed, not the rich? I wonder how it was that the church conformed to the things of this world. More often than not it just seems to ape the hierarchical structures that one finds in many secular fields of employment. And another thing, why is it that the church seems to be so wealthy? Just look at its buildings, investments and art treasures and Jesus categorically says, 'do not store up for yourselves treasure on earth, where moth and rust destroy, and thieves break in and steal; but store up treasure in heaven, where neither moth nor rust will destroy, nor thieves break in and steal, For where your treasure is, there will your heart be also'. (Matt. 6; 19-21)

I must say Zeno, I am really impressed. I never knew that you were familiar with the bible. Unfortunately you have gone off the rails again and this is not the place to give a lesson in church history!

I want to emphasise that the important thing about this idea of service is not that the over-ambitious will be punished by having to do menial jobs, nor that those who want to rise in the hierarchy must do menial tasks. On the contrary, it is the service itself that is at the heart of the Christian community. As Manson wrote many years ago, 'in the Kingdom of God service is not a stepping-stone to nobility; it is nobility, the only kind of nobility that is recognised'. (10) Certainly Jesus does not use force in his own ministry. One could argue that he lets himself be killed rather than answer the violence of his enemies with his own violence. Retaliation of this kind is simply not on the agenda. That is the authority of Jesus. 'It is a *paradoxical authority* to the very last, an authority which in its unprotectedness and vulnerability turns any other type of authority upside down.' (11)

Z: I have to say I feel very vulnerable as a clown sometimes. People don't laugh and I wonder if I'm in the right job. Perhaps I have got it all wrong and I should be a juggler instead. Anyway, are there any other characteristics of the Kingdom?

Another characteristic of the kingdom, which is present in the teaching of Jesus, Fuellenback says, is eating with his disciples and the wider community. 'Meals were his favourite means to demonstrate the future of the Kingdom having already arrived with him.' (12) People found themselves eating with people in a new kind of community. 'The Son of Man came eating and drinking, and they say,'Look, a glutton and a drunkard, a friend of tax-collectors and sinners!'" (Matt. 11:19, Luke 7:34)

In Mark, which is the oldest of the gospels, there is a reference to Jesus sitting at dinner and 'many tax-collectors and sinners were also sitting with Jesus and his disciples'. (Mark 2: 15) It is not just that Jesus is eating, but it is the company he is keeping. Indeed, a further criterion of the Kingdom is that it seems to include those who have previously been excluded from society. The ministry of Jesus is distinctly biased towards children, the poor, the sick and those who were generally thought to be on the margins of society, 'the outcast, the disenfranchised, the despised and rejected.' (13)

Z: Yes, I have heard it said that a major complaint about Jesus was the company he kept.

That's exactly right. In Luke's gospel, as a prelude to the parables of the lost sheep, the lost coin and the lost sons, we read, "and the Pharisees and the scribes were grumbling and saying, 'this fellow welcomes sinners and eats with them'. " (Luke 15: 2) The parables that follow, Dutney maintains, are an explanation of Jesus' 'extraordinary and offensive practice of indiscriminate table fellowship'. (14) This practice is famously illustrated when he invites himself to tea at the house of the infamous tax-collector, Zacchaeus. (Luke 19:

1-10) Once again there is the familiar complaint. 'All who saw it began to grumble and said, "He has gone to be the guest of one who is a sinner".'

Z: I quite like the idea of eating being important! I'm rather fond of chocolate and cream cakes, not to mention custard pies, but I don't suppose there is any of that in the New Testament.

I think not! Incidentally a contemporary novel which is relevant to this theme is Chocolat. The heroine is ostracised by the local church because she dares to open a chocolate shop in a certain French village during the season of Lent. She then incurs the anger of the villagers because of the strange company she keeps. A film called Babette's feast is also very interesting. Babette lives with a very austere and joyless family but she prepares for them a magnificent banquet, a feast. The family are slowly transformed into a joyful community. However, returning to the bible we find the use of the imagery of feasting referring to the Kingdom has its origins in the Old Testament where God offers a banquet on Mount Zion for all people. For example, in Isaiah, 'on this mountain the Lord of hosts will make for all people a feast of rich food, a feast of well-matured wines, of rich food filled with marrow, of well-matured wines strained clear'. (25:6) This imagery is adopted in the New Testament especially in the parables where the Kingdom of God is likened to an invitation to a feast. (Matt. 22: 1-10, Luke 14: 16-24) People reject the invitation to attend the banquet for perfectly good reasons. They all have understandable excuses and so once again within the terms of the parable it is those on the margins of society who are invited, 'the poor, the crippled, the blind, and the lame'. (Luke 14: 21) Others found on the roads and the lanes were also invited. One can only imagine that the times of table fellowship were occasions of great fun and joy because those who had previously been excluded were now included.

Z: Do I detect here echoes of circus, fun, laughter, excitement, anticipation and celebration?

Absolutely. Sinners were being welcomed home, they were being affirmed. Hospitality and the sharing of food is a great indication that someone is valued and loved. The wedding banquet is also a symbol of the imminence of the Kingdom and Jesus is taken to task because his disciples do not fast like the Pharisees or the followers of John the Baptist. (Mark 2: 18-20, see also Matt. 8:11,12 and Luke 13: 28-29) Of course, the host of the banquet is Jesus himself.

It is interesting to note that many, though not all, of the resurrection appearances take place in the context of a meal. The most obvious example is the two disciples on the road to Emmaus who do not recognise the stranger who had joined them. His identity only becomes apparent as they gather found a table to eat a meal and the stranger breaks bread. (Luke 24: 13-32) Other examples where the risen Lord appears at a meal table are in the upper room (Luke 24: 36-43), as the eleven were sitting at table (Mark 16:14), by the lakeside (John 21: 1-14), and Luke records specifically that witnesses ate and drank with the risen Lord. (Acts 10:41) The meal table seems to become the place par excellence where one can encounter the risen Lord. 'The distinctively Christian ritual, breaking bread together, is coupled in the New Testament with the distinctively Christian affirmation, Jesus is risen.' (15)

Z: It is a bit different today when people gather round a box in the corner! The music for Coronation Street doesn't have the same effect as the affirmation 'the Lord is risen'!

Obviously, that wasn't a problem for the early Christians! They wanted to ensure that the work of Jesus continued, albeit eventually ritualised, in the Eucharistic celebration. Certainly in the Methodist tradition the Lord's Supper, or Eucharist, has been celebrated with an 'open' table at which all are welcome. The host at any such celebration is the risen Lord, it is his table, not the church's. It seems out of keeping with the gospel tradition to limit those who can receive bread and wine to those who have previously given some kind of public commitment, usually, in the form of a confirmation service. Jesus invites all to come to sup and eat with him and to discriminate on grounds decided upon by the church contravenes that specific invitation of Jesus. Indeed, as we have seen, a criterion for the Kingdom of God is not only that of eating round a table, but also a resistance to the exercise of power and a distinct positive bias in favour of those who one would not normally invite. Not only that but all will eat and be satisfied, as in the feeding of the 5000 and the feeding of the 4000.

Z: I like the idea of everyone eating and everyone being satisfied. In all honesty how can I eat, drink and feel really satisfied when other people haven't anything to eat at all and have to walk miles for water?

Quite so. There is certainly evidence to suggest that the early disciples carried on the tradition of eating together. This is well attested in the Acts of the Apostles where 'they devoted themselves to the apostles' teaching and fellowship, to the breaking of bread and the prayers.' (2:42). The theme of acceptance was also carried on by Paul in his well known all usive verse, 'There is no longer Jew or Greek, there is no longer slave or free, there is no longer male or female; for all of you are one in Christ Jesus.' (Gal 3: 28) Peter struggled with this idea of inclusiveness until a decisive moment in the life of the early church. He had a vision whilst, interestingly, food was being prepared. (Acts 10) In the vision he sees a variety of animals which a voice invites him to kill and eat. Peter replied, 'by no means, Lord; for I have never eaten anything that is profane or unclean'. The voice speaks a second time, 'what God has made clean, you must not call profane'. The meaning eventually became clear to Peter. He realised that the gospel was not only for the Jews but also for the Gentiles. He was actually called to the house of a gentile, the Roman centurion, Cornelius and Peter began to see that God has no favourites, 'God shows no partiality, but in every nation anyone who fears him and does what is right is acceptable to him'. (10:34) As with Jesus, Peter is interrogated 'the circumcised believers criticised him, saying, 'Why did you go to uncircumcised men and eat with them?" (11:3) Peter was at pains to explain his vision but the controversy raised its head again at the Council of Jerusalem. (Acts 15: 1-29) The question of whether to include Gentiles or not would not easily go away.

In the end the matter was resolved with the condition that Gentiles were accepted into the community if they 'abstain from what has been sacrificed to idols and from blood and from what is strangled'. (Acts 15:29) Once again it appears that food played an important part in the early church. However, the over riding condition for acceptance into the fellowship was faith in Jesus. He is the one who receives sinners and forgives them. Sadly one does not have to go far into Christian history to discover those who have hurt, tortured or even killed other people, supposedly, in the name of Christianity. Even some were killed or excluded because they did not hold to the more orthodox beliefs of the church. Those on the margins have often been regarded as sinners and beyond the pail. In the past women have been excluded from holding many offices in the church, supremely from being ordained. Today the Anglican Church is in danger of being split asunder by its contrasting attitudes towards gay and lesbian Christians. There is an ambiguous attitude towards those of other Faiths. Are they a lost cause or should Christians engage in dialogue with people of other Faiths? Finally, the church has been exclusively male and hierarchical over the years and therefore not a good example of the community that Jesus had in mind. It need hardly be said the church can never be equated with the Kingdom of God. 'The church is, therefore, not the Kingdom now, because the Kingdom makes itself felt outside the church as well. The church's mission is to serve the Kingdom, not to take its place.' (16)

Z: In the circus we struggle with many issues and I'm sure it must have been the same for the first Christians. My question is about authority. It is all very well to say that in the Kingdom of God there is no dominance and power only service but might this not lead to anarchy if no one is in charge? We have a ringmaster or mistress in charge of us and we have to take notice of what they say.

Of course, there was always apostolic authority but beyond that Paul introduces the concept of 'charisma'. The importance of this concept can be seen from the fact that as Käsemann says 'we can establish with the maximum degree of historical certainty' (17) that Paul was the first to use this word in a technical sense and to introduce it into the language of theology. The emergence of this word suggests that something important was happening within the Christian community and this could only be expressed by means of a new terminology.

Z: There you go again. As if we didn't have enough words in the English language you have to introduce another Greek one.

'Charismata' are spiritual gifts but they exist only to the extent that they are all related to the one 'charisma', the one gift, which is the gift of God and is 'eternal life in Christ Jesus our Lord'. (Roms 6:23) In 1 Cor. 12: 4ff 'diakonia' is interchangeable with 'charisma'. The gift must move one to action and it is this action or service which is the outward manifestation of the inner 'charisma'. But 'charismata' can be misused, as in Corinth. There can even be false apostles. (2 Cor. 11:13)

Z: How do you know whether a particular spiritual gift is genuine or not?

Such spirits must be tested, and Paul, in the context of ecclesiastical order and authority, gives his solution. (1 Cor.14) For him the test of a genuine 'charisma' lies not in the fact that something supernatural has happened but in the use to which it is put. A 'charisma' can only be authenticated by the service that issues from it. This service must be in the service of Christ and 'edify' or 'build up' the community. Within the community there is a diversity of 'charimata' and they all constitute the body of Christ. 'The body does not consist of one member but of many. ' (1Cor.12:14) Moreover, this diversity does not, or should not, lead to the disintegration of the body but just the opposite, it makes true unity possible. If all are endowed with the same gifts, then there would be too much of that particular ability but if all have different gifts, mutual service is the result. The same chapter also warns that not too much prominence should be given to some members so that others are overshadowed and reduced to silence. There is room only for the domination of Christ. This unity of the body under Christ comes into existence through baptism (1 Cor. 12:13, Gal. 3:27) but it is a unity that becomes a reality in the act of service.

Z: I think I am beginning to get your drift but can you lighten up a bit?

There is no doubt that being a solitary Christian would not have made sense to the early Christians. In the Acts of the Apostles there is ample evidence of them meeting together for prayer and for a meal. Certainly Jesus often goes away to a solitary place to pray and being personally known by God and knowing God is central to the bible, but there is the well known verse 'for where two or three are gathered in my name, I am there among them'. (Matt. 18:20) God is present when people are gathered in his name.

Paul recognises a whole series of 'charismata', ranging from apostles, prophets and teachers to miracle-workers, those who speak in tongues and those having the gift of healing. ( 1 Cor. 12:28) To this list could be added those who give charity and help to those in distress (Rom. 12:8) and who help widows. (1 Tim.5:9ff) It is important to notice that it is not only the more outstanding services that count as charismatic. This is demonstrated by Paul's use of such expressions as 'according to the grace given to us' followed by a catalogue of gifts (Roms.12: 3ff) and 'each has a particular gift from God, one having one kind and another a different kind.' (1 Cor. 7:7) Therefore, whatever is mentioned in the same context as these expressions, for example, the condition of circumcised or uncircumcised, of free people or slave, must also be counted as 'charismata'. On further inspection of I Corinthians chapter 7 it can be seen that the scope of the concept becomes even wider because here, marriage and virginity are introduced as 'charismata'. The same pattern occurs elsewhere (Gal. 3:28) with the addition of 'male and female' and is further widened in another epistle. (Col. 3:11) The point is, as previously noted, that a genuine 'charisma' lies not in the fact of its existence but in the use to which it is put. The conditions of being male or female, or being involved in family life and relationships, of being sexually committed or virgin, of standing under or outside the Law, are not in themselves charismatic but they can become so 'in Christ'.

Z: It seems to me that just about anything can be viewed as charismatic but we seem to have moved along way from my question about authority.

For Paul, all Christians have a special 'charisma' and therefore a special responsibility. No individual possessor of a 'charisma' has a special prerogative over against other members of the Body of Christ. All are bearers of the Word of God and contribute to the building up of the community. Even the apostle, as Paul continually emphasises, is only one charismatic among many, though he may be the most important. There is a considerable measure of agreement among scholars that in the early church all were office-bearers, and therefore, in a sense, none were. Hanson refers to the search for some kind of ministerial pattern in the New Testament as a 'wild goose chase'. 'There is no single form or pattern of ministry exclusively authorised for the church by the New Testament. The only approximation to permanent officials are the Twelve, and even here it may be quite misleading to describe them as "officials".(18)

What we do find in the New Testament is a mutuality, a loving of each other, 'love one another with mutual affection' (Roms. 12:10), 'live in harmony with one another'
(Roms. 12:16). Christians are 'able to instruct one another' (Roms. 15:14), and they are exhorted to 'greet one another with a holy kiss'.
(Roms 16:16)

Z: Now this is getting interesting!

Members are to wait for one another before they eat (1 Cor. 11:33) and to 'have the same care for one another'. (1 Cor. 12.25) The freedom they have gained in Christ they are not to indulge in but 'through love become slaves to one another' (Gal. 5:13), and 'bear one another's burdens'. (Gal. 6:2) They are to 'encourage one another and build up each other', and 'to respect any who labour among you ..... esteem them very highly in love because of their work' and 'see that none of you repays evil for evil, but always seek to do good to one another and to all'. ( 1 Thess. 5: 11,13,15)

Z: So at the end of the day it all comes down to love?

I think that's about it in a nutshell but forgiveness is also of paramount importance.
To forgive is to set a prisoner free and discover the prisoner was you. (Matt. 6:14, 15)
Forgiveness is also something to do with forgetfulness. As Paul says, 'love keeps no record of wrongs'. (1 Cor. 13)

Z: I can't resist telling the following that I read in The Song of The Bird by Anthony de Mello. (19)

"Why do you keep talking about my past mistakes?" said the husband. "I thought you had forgiven and forgotten".

"I have, indeed, forgiven and forgotten," said the wife. "But I want to make sure you don't forget that I have forgiven and forgotten."

Very funny Zeno but you do have a point. It is said that God has no memory, but let me continue. Members of the early Christian community were to bear 'with one another in love' and 'be kind to one another, tender-hearted, forgiving one another, as God in Christ has forgiven you' and to be 'subject to one another out of reverence to Christ'. (Eph. 4: 2,32; 5:32) These sentiments are reiterated elsewhere, 'bear with one another and, if anyone who has a complaint against another, forgive one another; just as the Lord has forgiven you, so you also must forgive. Above all, clothe yourselves with love, which binds everything together in perfect harmony.' (Col. 3: 13,14) These themes continue in the first letter of Peter. 'Maintain constant love for one another, for love covers a multitude of sins. Be hospitable to one another without complaining. ....serve one another with whatever gift each of you has received.' (1Peter 4: 7-10) Not only forgiveness and love are paramount but members need to confess their sins to each other and to pray for each other. (James 5:16)

Z: I'm not too happy about that. I thought I could just confess to God. That is hard enough. Anyway, if I started to confess my sins to somebody they would need to have a lot of spare time!

I think people were much more open to each other in days gone by, than they are now. Clearly, there was a kind of togetherness in the early community, a very positive attitude towards each other. These communities were called 'ekklesia' and simply referred to the assemblies of fellow Christians. Confusion abounds because in the New Testament 'ekklesia' is the Greek word used for church and some have argued that church is another way of saying the Kingdom of God.

Z: I'm glad it's not just me who gets confused.

The church is not the same as the Kingdom of God. The latter is far bigger than the church.

A Greek word used to describe the early Christian communities was 'Koinonia' meaning a community of sharing, 'having all things in common ('koina'), and the word referred primarily to the practices of the early Christian gatherings. It also seems to have referred to some kind of 'fellowship' of sharing, some sense of participation in a common task'. (20) It could well be argued that members of these gatherings looked after each other and were drawn together because of the hostile world in which they found themselves . They had, as it were, a common enemy. Perhaps for this reason Paul's letters seem to devote themselves almost exclusively with what it entails to be a member of the fellowship. As we have seen there is more a ministry of building up each other rather than a ministry to the world around them. We would call these communities today counter cultural in that they are not taking their lead from the surrounding secular society. Lohfink calls them contrast societies. 'Precisely to the degree that the people of God let itself be grasped by God's rule it would be transformed…it would become a contrast-society. This in no way meant that it would become a theocratic state, but rather that it would become a family of brothers and sisters, just like the family Jesus had gathered in his circle of disciples.' (21)

Z: So we are back to the idea of family.

Love is very much the recurring theme in these communities. When the church at Corinth is tearing itself apart with internal disputes Paul wrote to them his celebrated hymn to love. (1 Cor. 13) But this love is not a theoretical concept, it manifestes itself in practical ways. 'There was not a needy person among them, for as many owned lands or houses sold them and brought the proceeds of what was sold…it was distributed to each as any had need.' (Acts 4: 34-35) Furthermore Paul asked the Corinthians to put money aside on the first day of every week so that he could collect it on arrival and take it to the church in Jerusalem.
(1 Cor. 16: 1-4)

Z: This love certainly showed itself in action.

I hope you are getting the idea about the corporate nature of the church and the notion of Christian community. I have given you a very quick introduction to the idea of Christian community as found in the New Testament. I hope you now realise that the Kingdom of God is an important concept along with its characteristics of service and non domination, the importance of food or gathering round a table for fellowship and the importance of including those who might be regarded as being on the edges of society. These communities tried to live by the precept of love and forgiveness and mutual caring and support. Questions remain. How did these communities see their mission to the world? Did not John envisage God as sending Jesus into the world because He loved it? (John 3:16) Where does the final command of Matthew's gospel come in, the command to go into all the world and make disciples of all nations? (Matt: 28:19) If these communities were so pre-occupied with themselves was there not a danger that they would remain a sect and therefore have nothing to say to the secular world?

It is beyond my remit to try to answer these questions in depth. At one level there is an obvious answer. The apostles themselves, especially Paul, travelled around the known world in order to try to establish Christian communities in which people could live out their lives of faithfulness to Jesus. This is a known fact, proof of which is found in the Acts of the Apostles along with Paul's various letters. However, it is a matter of debate as to how long these communities continued before they began to conform to the world. They were very radical in their approach and tried to follow the teachings of Jesus as closely as they could, but it is unlikely they survived after the church was given official recognition by the Emperor Constantine. What did begin to emerge were communities established around the Desert Fathers and these eventually gave rise to the Monastic movement.

Z: But what does all this mean for the church today?

## Points to Ponder:

1. The characteristics of a Christian community as found in the New Testament include: service, non domination, eating together, including those on the margins of society, living lives of love and forgiveness, mutual caring and support. To what extent are these characteristics found in your local church?

2. Of the above characteristics which do you think you need to do more about in your own life as a Christian?

3. What do you think Jesus would say today about women in positions of authority in the church?

4. Although Jesus doesn't say anything in the gospels about gay people what do you think he might say today?

5. How important for you is it to sit round a table and eat with family and friends?

6. How difficult do you find it to forgive someone?

## Meditation:

Tea in the Desert

Wandering, alone, through the desert.
Sun shrieking heat,
Sweat pouring and dripping,
Rocks, barren and hostile
Sheltering.
The brave desert flower.
And I-solitary beating heart
In a vast and empty land
Wandering, wandering, seeking
A lost and lonely God.

Beyond the rocks
A smell of goats
Hanging thick and sweet
In the still air.

And there, standing defiant against
A thousand miles of sand,
A woman
Burnt brown, clad
In sweeping black and
Coloured beads.

We walk to meet,
To cross
The centuries and the nations.
Eyes, black, shining a lost
And ancient wisdom
Speaking the naked horrors
And splendour of
Uncompromising solitude.

Smile. No words.
Shattering the barriers of language.
Hands touch,
Brown and cracked,
White and smooth,
Clasping and joining
A thousand cultures.

Walk together to her home
A rough and sturdy shelter
Of rocks and goatskins.
Squat on Tuareg run laid out
Proudly on the sand.
Smile. No words.

Eyes, searching, speaking
A million unknown words.
Tea. Thick, hot, sweet

Prepared with love and care
In an old tin kettle
On an open fire.
Sip. Smile gratitude.
Smile. No words.

Woman of the desert.
Woman of the West.
The world brought together.
Peace and harmony established.
Rivalry and hate abolished.
Black and white.
The lion and the lamb.
Smile. No words.
Tuareg woman.
English woman.
Sharing the Kingdom.
Sipping tea
In the vast and lonely desert
With a found and
Living God.( 22)

## References

1. Lohfink, Gerhard, <u>Jesus and Community,</u> SPCK 1985, p.8
2. ibid. p.17
3. ibid. p.29
4. ibid., p.10
5. ibid.
6. Reid, J.K.S., <u>The biblical doctrine of the Ministry,</u> Oliver & Boyd, Edinburgh and London 1955, p.5

7. Campenhausen, Hans von, Ecclesiastical authority and spiritual power in the church of the first three centuries, Adam & Charles Black, London 1969, p.14

8. Chilton, Bruce, Pure Kingdom, Jesus' Vision of God, SPCK 1996, p.8

9. Lohfink, op. cit., p.115

10. Manson,T.W., The Church's Ministry, Hodder & Stoughton, London 1948, p.27

11. Lohfink, op. cit., p.117

12. Fuellenbach, John, The kingdom of God, the message of Jesus today, Orbis, New York 1995, p.95

13. Dutney, Andrew, Food, sex and death, a personal account of Christianity, Uniting Church Press, Melbourne 1993, p.67

14. ibid.

15. ibid., p.75

16. Fuellenbach., op. cit., p.266

17. Käsemann, Ernst, Essays on New Testament themes, SCM, London 1964, p.64

18. Hanson,R.P.C., Groundwork for Unity, SPCK, London 1971, p.17

19. de Mello, Anthony, The Song of the Bird, Image Books, 1984, p.123

20. Hanson, Paul, The people called: the growth of community in the bible, Harper & Row 1986, p.14

21. Lohfink, op. cit., p.72

22. Gately, Edwina, Psalms of a Lay Woman, Anthony Clarke, 1986

# Chapter12

## CHURCH MUSINGS

Z: Don't you mean church amusings?

Not at all. I'm being very serious. A few days ago it was the season of Epiphany. Naturally, therefore, the preacher for the Sunday service took the theme of the wise men from the East visiting the baby Jesus. Again, quite naturally, the congregation sang
'Brightest and best are the sons of the morning,
            Dawn on our darkness and lend us thine aid;
Star of the East, the horizon adorning,
            Guide where our infant Redeemer is laid.

The hymn goes on to talk about 'odours of Edom', and 'ample oblation'.

Z: Say no more. You've lost me!

It is wonderful imagery but it was written at the beginning of the 19th Century. As I joined in the singing, I really, really struggled to enter into the thought forms of 200 years ago. The music was written round about the same time and therefore in a completely different musical idiom from that pertaining today. Music has evolved through the ages. William Walton or Vaughan Williams could no more have written their music in Beethoven's time as could Beethoven have composed his works before Henry Purcell. Now, I am a great lover of Beethoven but such classical music in a pop culture does not go down well.

A wonderful occasion took place earlier this year when there was a concert called 'Dr. Who at the proms'.

Z: <u>Who</u> did you say?

I think you heard right the first time! A wonderfully mixed audience, although predominantly young people, were introduced to orchestral music at the Royal Albert Hall. It was an excellent concert, pulsating with life, vigour, energy, laughter and good music. My guess is that only a handful of the young people would have turned up if the programme had been solely the music of Beethoven.

In church, we continue to sing the 'old classics' but they have no appeal, or meaning to younger people. The hymns of Isaac Watts and the Wesleys no longer resonate with the youth of today. More importantly, God is not stuck in the thought forms of 250 years ago. He continues to reveal himself and so we have to worship him in ways that are appropriate for today. Any relationship, if it is to grow, changes over the years. Some things stay the same but others change. Although my wife is the same person I married and to that extent she is the same, nevertheless, her needs, and mine, have changed over the years.

Z: I think your wife is lovely and she certainly has a lot of patience putting up with you but don't forget she also has another personality – Lucia de Lammamour. Lucia and me have a double act. She is a natural.

You are getting completely off the point. I was talking about change not about you and your clowning.

Z: That reminds me of the time you told me about when you went as a student to preach in a Yorkshire chapel. You said to the old steward that you must have seen a lot of changes. His reply was "Ay lad, and I've resisted everyone of 'em".

I recently attended a church service and none of the five hymns that had been chosen had been written in the twentieth century let alone the twenty first. Do I want to visit a doctor who is basing her remedies on medical practice of the eighteenth century? Surely not. In the same way I want to worship God in the language and thought forms of today. God is not locked in the past. Either God is alive today, in some form or another, or dead without trace.

Z: I have the advantage of not being recognised when I am not dressed in my clown clothes and I often take a quick look at faces of the congregation as they sing. When the hymns are from a different age, I often get the distinct impression that people are singing out of a sense of duty or obligation rather than a sense of passion. Their lips are mouthing the words but their hearts are not in it. This seems far removed from the central notion of worship as celebration. All of us have been affected by changes in our daily lives – television, computers, central heating, vacuum cleaners, micro wave cookers, shopping malls, supermarkets, cars, high speed travel, package holidays and so on. What changes in a life time! Yet there is the feeling in church that 'nothing changes here'.

My local butcher now sells a huge variety of pizzas, burgers and kebabs, not to mention a whole list of exotic sausages, a selection that would have been unthinkable a generation ago. The moral of the story is that if one doesn't change in keeping with the times then one is doomed to perish and that, sadly, is what has happened to many local shops. They have been unable to keep up with the competition from the supermarkets. Many churches have perished because they thought they could just carry on in the face of the facts and just hope there is going to be some kind of religious revival. For many the competition from garden centres, Sunday shopping, sports centres, sporting events, car boot sales and family visits has proved irresistible. Of course, Sunday services were doomed as soon as a television became a fixture in most homes. Who, in the sixties, could resist the temptation from staying in to watch the latest episode of The Forsyte Saga? Wasn't it much cosier to stay at home and watch Songs of Praise rather than sit in a cold church on a hard pew? Our culture has shifted dramatically in a generation and churches ignore it at their peril.

I once visited someone and before I left he showed me his pride and joy – a beautiful vintage car, gleaming from top to bottom, in his garage. This was a wonderful example of how people used to travel in bygone days. Today it would be lovely to go in it for a gentle cruise round some country lanes but absolutely useless for travelling a long distance. This car was constructed for slow, sedate travel, not the fast lanes of motorways. In its day it was the bee's knees but now, nothing more than a museum piece. A very interesting museum piece, indeed, a much sought after collector's item but not equipped for present day requirements.

Z: I don't think you would get very far in that old banger you bought for £50 years ago.

Somebody said to me the other day that she wanted to pass on to the next generation all that she held dear about Methodism. I wonder what it is that she would want to pass on. We all have an idea what is meant by the phrase 'the treasures of Methodism' and so I am not going to define what I mean. Suffice it to say that I have been part of Methodism all my life and have never wanted to be part of another church. I cherish the tradition I was brought up and would very much like my offspring to be part of that same tradition. Therein lies the problem. Let me offer an illustration.

My wife, Lucy, and I, own a lovely old clock which sits proudly on our mantelpiece and chimes away from time to time with its distinctive musical notes. For my wife especially this sound recalls memories of childhood when that very same clock sat on her grandma's mantelpiece. It has been passed on to Lucy as a family heirloom. She would dearly love to pass it on to one of our family. Suppose none of them want it. This could be for a variety of reasons. It doesn't have the same memories or it is simply too old fashioned, or it just does not fit in with their décor at home, or they prefer a modern digital clock to a numerical one.

In the above paragraph simply substitute the phrase 'treasures of Methodism' or 'treasures of the church' for the word clock and you will see what the problem is. The younger generation is simply not interested in what I so dearly want to pass on. For this reason I get a little frustrated sometimes when people enthuse about anything to do with Wesley – John or Charles. Of course, they are vital to my faith but what can I pass on? Do I pass on an old fashioned clock which will surely be consigned to the dustbin because it is no earthly use to any one? Without doubt I can continue to listen to my clock and my treasures but the task for me is to work out how to 'serve the present age' as Wesley himself wrote in one of his hymns. This is a challenge that is sometimes not taken up because we are so busy maintaining our treasures to the extent that they are in danger of becoming museum pieces. My calling as a Christian, let alone a minister, is not to be the curator of a museum.

Z: Before long you will be old enough to be displayed in a museum!!

The new wine of the good news of the gospel always needs to be expressed in contemporary ways otherwise the intoxicating effect of the good news is lost. As Jesus said, 'one puts new wine into fresh wineskins'. (Mark 2:22 ) Failure to do this results in burst wine skins and therefore the wine is lost. The gospel always has to be expressed in ways that are appropriate to a given culture at any given time.

In case you think I am overstating my case please note that I recently went to a Methodist ordination service. Two of the hymns we sang, although they are in the Methodist hymn book, I have never chosen during 40 years of leading worship. The concepts illustrated were important but they were not stated in ways that expressed my spirituality let alone that of future generations.

If the clock cannot be passed on, then the problem is to find something that can be passed on. Can the thing that Lucy and I want our children to inherit be expressed in other ways? Perhaps we shall have to buy them another time piece that they can treasure because they know it is from us. Spending time with family would give them things to remember and that would produce its own souvenirs. The old clock is a souvenir of stability, love, care and home; feelings of a safe childhood. Our children have their own things that remind them of those feelings. They have been passed on.

There is a danger of thinking the thing that we pass on is important, for example, a Wesley hymn, but it is what the hymn represents that is important. The clock of itself is not important; rather what it represents, that is, a connection with Lucy and me and with our experiences. It is, or could be, a statement of our Christian faith and Christian vitality. Is there another way of passing on that important faith experience with which the next generation could more easily connect?

For all traditional Methodists, and thank God there are lots of them, the task is to work out ways of passing on all that they hold dear. That means finding ways of connecting with the younger generation.

Z: I guess that when you do what you always do, you get what you always get.

All that has been said of music and hymns can be said of doctrine. It is heretical of me to say so but the church repeatedly boxes itself into a corner with regard to doctrine. Different denominations do it in slightly different ways but the result is the same. If you believe things in the way we do, if you do things the way we do them, then you are one of us and you can sign on the dotted line. If, on the other hand, you disagree with us, then you are decidedly not one of us and you must be excluded from our church. In this way churches become very tribal and very exclusive. A classic case would be arguments that have taken place about communion wine; should it be red or white, fermented or unfermented, should we drink from a chalice or small, separate communion glasses? How frequently should we celebrate communion? Every time we worship, weekly, monthly or not at all?

Z: No doubt if Jesus had been born in China he would have used rice in which case there would have been arguments about long grained or short grained, brown or white, basmatic or whatever.

Now I am a great believer in God being a God who delights in our diversity but does this mean that we have to engrave in concrete one particular denominational brand? The unconscious conclusion is that because I am a Methodist, say, then because God loves me he must like Methodists and therefore, it goes without saying, that God is a Methodist as well! Of course, this works for all denominations simply because we believe the one we are in to be the right one.

Z: So God isn't a Methodist then?

God is non-denominational! I think he is also the God of Jews and Muslims but that is a slightly different point. The problem is that we think our path up the mountain is the only one but in reality there are many paths. There are many ways to climb Snowdon, the highest mountain in Wales and I have tried many of them, but they are all different, presenting different challenges, different terrain, different levels of difficulty and different views. Throughout history people seem not only intent on creating their own path but also saying that it is the right path.

Z: Dear Lord, forgive me for thinking I am right and everybody else is wrong!

It could well be argued that the ecumenical movement is working hard to counter this divisiveness. To a certain extent that is absolutely true. I was minister of a church in Petersfield, Hampshire, and there, 'churches together' were involved in twenty different projects. These ranged from the usual walk of witness on Good Friday and the annual carol service to the setting up of a counselling service, a bookshop and a youth centre. The town was quite remarkable for the way in which Christians from all denominations were able to work together in a variety of different ways. My fear is that the movement has gone as far as it can go. Even if present disagreements on doctrines are overcome there are still big institutional issues to work through. If there was ever one Church, who would own the buildings that are now denominational and who would pay the clergy and what would happen to the pension funds?

Z: I can see why you might be worried about your pension!

These are major questions to do with our organizations. Let me add a caveat. To be one Church does not mean that we all do the same thing. I like the analogy of a multiplex cinema. Everybody congregates in the same building and maybe some similar things occur like eating pop corn or ice cream but different films are viewed. People choose the film they wish to see and the time they wish to see it. This is a far cry from years ago when each town had a few different cinemas each showing just one film at one particular time. Could the multiplex be a model for the future Church?

Z: The church I went into actually had tip up seats!

All this, is notwithstanding the work of the ecumenical movement, which seeks to find common ground amongst denominations rather than division. Churches tend to be very exclusive and this is contrary to the teachings of Jesus. He is noted for his inclusiveness to such an extent that people become very uncomfortable. The righteous people of his day, the Pharisees, objected to the fact that Jesus ate with sinners. Not only that, but Jesus went out of his way to incorporate people on the margins of society. In his day both women and children had no status in society yet he goes out of his way to meet and include them. He puts a child in the midst of a group of people and says the Kingdom of God is like a child. He, a rabbi, does the unthinkable of talking to a woman in public, in broad daylight. If further proof is needed of Jesus' desire to include everybody, he goes to the house of a notorious tax gatherer for tea and he touches a leper.(Matt: 8:3) It cannot be overstated how far Jesus overstepped the social conventions of his day. For Jesus, no one was excluded from the Kingdom. All were invited. All were welcome. They didn't have to sign on a dotted line, or agree to certain doctrinal statements, or perform rituals in a particular kind of way. All people had to do was to respond to the invitation of Jesus, 'follow me'.

Z: You make it sound very easy!

In one sense it is, but don't forget that following implies movement! That is quite literally the sticking point and that is where people exclude themselves. They refuse to accept the invitation of Jesus. He tells a parable of how people all too often find something else to do rather than accept his invitation. They make excuses; a field has been bought and the owner needs to see it; a yoke of oxen have been bought and need tending; somebody else has just married and therefore, presumably, is far too preoccupied.(Luke 14:15ff) Excuses could be thought of today. I have just got married; I've bought a house/car; there's a programme on t.v. I can't possibly miss; my family are coming for lunch; I'm going to a car boot sale; I'm just too busy; I can't be bothered. The disappointment of those who miss the opportunity of going to the banquet is not recorded, but we are told that the invitation goes out to the highways and byways – to those on the margins of society. Again, we see how Jesus incorporated those on the margins in that people who were normally excluded, often through no fault of their own, were wholeheartedly included.

Z: Perhaps I could actually be included as well!

I certainly hope so. The ministry of Jesus seems to have been all inclusive except for those who excluded themselves. But even today, there are some sections of church life where women are excluded in various ways. This is not because of anything they have done but because of who they are! Children can easily be excluded because they make too much noise! In general, people like children in church but only when they are grown up. In some churches, gay people are excluded, often with great vehemence.

Z: Do you remember me telling you about the occasion I entered a central London church in my full clown outfit! All sorts of things went through my mind. Where shall I sit? As I enter, they have all got their backs to me. Perhaps, if I just sit at the back, no one will notice me. What will people think? I seem to be wearing different clothes to everybody else? Will I look stupid? Will people be embarrassed by my presence? When do I stand and when do I sit down? Which book do I use and which page are we on? Will it be acceptable for me to receive bread and wine? Will I be thrown out? Will anyone laugh at me?

Yes, I remember you telling me with lots of feeling. You were obviously in touch with many of the questions people think and feel when they go into church for the first time. Yet, church, on the face of it, is the place par excellence where people of all descriptions need to feel accepted. All are welcome is sometimes written in bold letters outside a church. Sadly, this is often not the case as the above list of questions illustrates. In many churches it is certainly a prerequisite that you can read because on entry you are handed a variety of hymn books, song sheets and service books. If you are white and middle class, entering a white middle class church, then all is fine and dandy. If you are something else, then questions, often unspoken, can arise, and the person can be left to feel very uncomfortable as the odd one out. Birds of a feather flock together and woe betides if you belong to a different flock.

The word belonging is very important. Whereas in former times, as stated above, you needed to sign on the dotted line to say you agreed with a certain set of doctrinal statements before you could actually belong, the situation has now reversed. People need to feel that they belong before they will go the whole hog of signing on the dotted line. This 'signing' is known variously as adult baptism, confirmation or becoming a member of the church. Now, at one time, this was a fairly obvious thing to do. It was the next step for people to make on their Christian journey. The emphasis was on the fact that it was the next step, not a final step. The journey was not complete. It was emphasized that this was a good thing to do – to make one's commitment to Christ and his Church public. Confirmation and the like is a public statement. 'This is who I want to follow'. In a similar way, marriage is a public commitment of a couple's love for each other. The marriage service contains the words 'before God and in the presence of us all, A and C have exchanged vows….'.

Z: How things have changed. At one time people married and then lived together but now, for many, they live together and then, possibly, get married.

The problem today is that just as people are hesitant to get married, so people are hesitant to stand up in public and 'join' a church. The word commitment can feel a bit threatening and imply a curtailment of one's liberty.

Z: The difference between involvement and commitment is the difference between ham and eggs. The pig is committed but the hen is merely involved.

There is a sense in which people feel they belong to the church but don't join. As long as it is there, then that Church is for them. They may get married there, have their children baptised and hope to have a funeral service there. Rather like people enjoy living in a democracy, but would never think of voting. People only notice something when it is no longer there.

There is also the ever present feeling that something else may turn up so better to keep options open, just in case. Maybe he/she is not the one for me. Even when people feel they belong there is the tendency to hedge one's bets. We live in a shop around culture where people are no longer loyal to a particular market brand. They simply want the best bargain. It does not matter which supermarket it is so long as the product is good and the best price. In similar fashion, people are not so much concerned about the denominational label over the door of the church but does it offer what they are looking for. I have often talked to people after a church service and discovered they are new to the area. They quite openly admit they are 'shopping around' to see what different churches have to offer. Previously it mattered a great deal whether a church was Methodist, Baptist , Church of England or whatever. The first thing people looked for was the brand name over the door or notice board. Now these distinctions are becoming blurred. Indeed, even within denominations there is not the uniformity that there once was. For example, a Methodist service tended to follow a fairly predictable pattern in all churches. Quite literally all congregations sang from the same hymn book. Now there is a variety of home made song books and praise books, different versions of the bible in the pews and different orders of service. In some churches people other than the minister may pray the intercessions, and read from the bible whilst in others it is all left in the hands of the one conducting the service. There can be a charismatic, evangelical, liberal or middle of the road theological flavour. There is a huge variety of different approaches. The same applies in many other denominations especially, perhaps, the Church of England.

The logical conclusion to all this variety is that, at the end of the day, I will just do my own thing. I will be a Christian in my own particular life style. No longer do I need to search for a particular church; I will be completely independent and, as it were, be my own church. This is individualism gone mad. Of paramount importance in the New Testament is the corporate idea of the church. There, the church is likened to a body, a vine, a building all of which imply that it is impossible to be a Christian on your own. The very thought would have been a contradiction in terms to the early Christians. The church, of its very essence, is a corporate body. At its heart, from the very beginning, is a group of people gathered round a table, eating a meal together. How can you be a Christian on your own?! As Paul says in his metaphor of the body, 'the body does not consist of one member but many'. ( 1 Cor. 12: 14)

Z: I'm all in favour of gathering round at a table and eating.

Jesus exhorts us to believe not only with our hearts – and that is really important – but also with our minds. Singers of Charles Wesley hymns are exhorted in their worship to become 'lost in wonder, love and praise', (HP 267) but also to 'work and speak and <u>think</u> for thee'. (HP 745) I am firmly of the belief that some Christians switch off there heads as soon as they enter Church. They stop thinking. A classic Christmas carol is 'away in a manger'. One line of it is 'but little Lord Jesus no crying he makes'. We all sing it with great feeling but I have yet to come across a baby that doesn't cry! Another Christmas example would be 'Once in royal David's city'. 'Christian children all must be, mild, obedient, good as he'. This is a very Victorian image of Jesus when little children should be seen and not heard. My image of Jesus is not that of someone who was mild. He did after all, overthrow the money changers in the temple with a considerable amount of anger and he had some very hard words to say to hypocrites. The carol continues with the image of Jesus in heaven, 'set at God's right hand on high'.

Z: Didn't the first astronauts say there couldn't possibly be a God because they hadn't found one up there in space?

Quite so, but it needs to be said that this observation of the astronaut is not an argument against God's existence. God is not located in any particular place. God is not one object amongst many others.

Of course, it could also be argued that some Christians continually switch off their hearts. There is no sense of energy or passion or enthusiasm about the Christian life. I sometimes enter a church service and feel a sense of deadness if not when I enter, then, when I leave!! I recently attended a morning service and left near to tears. The whole service had been so utterly boring. Where was the sense of expectancy, the sense of awe or the sense that this was an encounter with the Divine? God was simply not present. Who was it who said that every church should carry the sign outside 'you are entering a danger zone, hard hats must be worn'? It is no good wearing fur hats, straw hats or any other kind of hat. This is not a social club but a place where you are going to meet God and therefore anything could happen. Indeed, God might actually speak to you! That is the Christian belief. Where two or three are gathered together, there is God in the midst.

I fervently believe that God is where the life is. In the New Testament, the writer of the fourth gospel continually reiterates the theme that God is a God of life, epitomised in the life of Jesus. 'I am the resurrection and the life'. 'I am the way, the truth and the life'. 'I am the bread of life'. 'I have come that you may have life and enjoy it in all its abundance'. 'In Him was life'. Sadly, some churches have become so concerned with existing, with keeping going, they have lost their life and are preoccupied with blowing air into dead embers.

Z: Or dead members! I'm all for living life to the full.

Bill Shankly, a football manager, once famously remarked that football was much more important than life or death. In a way, so is the gospel of Jesus. There was something in the life of Jesus that was so compelling, so contagious, that his followers gave up everything in order to follow him and were even prepared to die for him. I fear that some of that contagion has been lost.

Z: Maybe some of the urgency and impact of the gospel has been lost because church members have become so concerned with the future of their own church that they have lost sight of their origins.

That could well be true. I talked about biblical ideas of community in the last chapter so let's see if they are relevant today.

An overarching theme in the early church was that of service. Undoubtedly there are many Christians who are engaged in lives of service and much of their work is completely unknown to the general public. For example, I can think of someone who has worked as a friend for the Samaritans all his life. In fact, he was one of the first Samaritans. This was a ministry of service which very few people knew about.

Z: No doubt you could give lots of other examples.

I certainly could. Many voluntary organizations would collapse if they were not supported by members from the local churches. It would be an interesting exercise for a local church to carry out an audit of how many of its members were involved in organizations which, in one way or another, served people in the community. This service could be seen as a direct consequence of their faith in God. I guess there is always room for churches to do more in the community but the church is something other than a community centre. I prefer the concept of church as a health centre – a place where people are accepted with no strings attached, where people can find wholeness of body, mind and spirit, a place where you can really be you in your full humanity, above all else, a place where people can find God.

Z: Just as a lot of power and authority can be invested in a medical doctor can the same be said of ministry?

Yes it can. However, there is no one pattern of ministry within the New Testament but one gets the impression that there was a sense of equality which is often missing today. Indeed there is a hierarchy and this can lead to a misuse of power and authority. I recently came across a vicar who was afraid of meeting his diocesan bishop because of the power that could be exerted over him.

Z: That seems to be an extreme example.

I'm not so sure about that. There is in the church a feeling that the ultimate authority must lie with the priest, or vicar or minister.

Z: Or pope.

Quite so. The concept of the Priesthood of All Believers, that great cry of the Reformation, is still being discovered. In other language we talk about the ministry of the 'whole people of God' but it is an ideal that we are still striving after. I heard recently of a local council of churches that always has to have an ordained person as its chair.

Z: Are the laity not good enough?

It would be very easy to jump to that conclusion. As we have seen, in some sections of the church women are, apparently, not good enough. Jesus, on the other hand, was at pains to bring people into his sphere of activity so that all were included. One of the problems in some churches is that people have been going for so long they know each other very well. They have been friends or acquaintances for many years. Without knowing it, they have formed a kind of in group and it is very difficult for new people to become part of that group.

Z: A question to ask, therefore, is whether the local church is genuinely inclusive or has it become a clique?

That is a very good question and particularly relevant in the light of the many people around who are from ethnic minorities. It is so easy to patronize, or to make assumptions. Many years ago I found myself sitting next to a West Indian in a college setting. We engaged in conversation and I asked him what is job was in the college. I hope my total surprise wasn't obvious when he told me he was the college principal.

Z: That really caught you out.

It did indeed but notice that we engaged in conversation because we were sitting round a table eating lunch. The meal had provided an opportunity to get to know someone at a different and deeper level. As we have seen eating together was a mark of the early church and therefore the question needs to be asked, how many opportunities are there for people in your church to get together for a meal?

Z: I guess this is all to do with the more general question of hospitality.

That's right, offering friendship and welcome to the stranger is a theme running through the bible. In the Old Testament there is the example of Abraham (Gen. 18) and many instructions to be hospitable (Ex. 23:9, Lev. 24:22) and even to be loving, thus imitating the love of God, 'you shall also love the stranger, for you were strangers in the land of Egypt.' (Deut 10:19) Exactly the same sentiment is taken up in the New Testament, 'extend hospitality to strangers'. (Roms, 12:13b) 'Do not neglect to show hospitality to strangers, for by doing that some have entertained angels unawares'. (Heb 13:2, see also Titus 1:8 and 1 Peter 4:9)

Z: All of which is easier said than done my friend. Who knows what might happen today if you let a complete stranger into your house?

I agree. One has to be careful. However, the pendulum seems to have gone too far in the direction of caution and it is relatively easy to exercise hospitality whilst at the same time ensuring precautions are in place. Offering hospitality is not only a way of building bridges it is a way of mending bridges, a way of offering forgiveness.

The question is about mutual care and support. Sometimes I have known people who have been faithful members of a group for many years and then, for some reason, they have been unable to attend. Weeks have gone by and nobody has thought to follow them up and ask the reason for their absence.

Z: So much for care and support.

Exactly. My final comment is around the question of whether people's 'gifts' are fully utilized in the church community? Where are the people who will take time to think 'outside the box' about the direction the church is taking? There are usually people who are willing to exercise their gifts by 'doing' things but where are the prophets who can look with insight into what is happening in the world and the church and reflect on the direction God wants them to take?

Z: Ah yes, blue sky thinking.

Something like that. As somebody has said if we are totally wrapped up in maintenance and 'keeping the show on the road', then there is no possibility of new ventures, no possibility of discerning God's way ahead.

Of course, the church, like everything else is affected by the culture in which it is set.

Z: Yes, but didn't someone say we have to be in the world but not of the world?

That may well be true, Christians have to be countercultural or, in the words of Paul, 'do not be conformed to this world, but be transformed by the renewing of your minds, so that you may discern what is the will of God – what is good and acceptable and perfect.' (Roms. 12:2)

Z: Again, that sounds easier said than done.

Agreed. There is a strong pull in many people to be like everybody else and not try to swim against the current.

Z: So where does all this leave the church of the future?

## Points to Ponder:

1.  What are the things in your life that are life giving? - deadening?

2.  What are the things in your church/community that are life giving? - deadening?

3.  What have been the major changes in your life?

4.  What have been the major changes in your church/ community?

5.  How many risks has your church taken recently?

## Meditation:

Take a piece of paper and a pencil/biro/paints. What is life like for you at the moment? Draw a picture depicting life for you. Where is God in your picture?

# Chapter 13

## WHITHER THE CHURCH?

Z: I hope you don't mean wither the church.

Certainly not. Some may say that the church is withering before our very eyes but that does not mean that the church will cease to exist. One thing is clear, the centre of gravity of Christendom, not for the first time, is moving away from the Western World. In Africa and parts of Asia like Korea, the church is growing at a rapid rate.

Z: This is all very well but where does that leave the church in the West?

During World War II a German pastor called Bonhoeffer was imprisoned by the Nazis. He wrote some letters from his prison cell among which is the following observation. 'We are proceeding towards a time of no religion at all: men as they are now simply cannot be religious any more'. (1)

Z: That must have been written well over sixty years ago.

I know. It is amazing. He goes on to say, 'If we reach the stage of being radically without religion – and I think this is more or less the case already, else how is it, for instance, that this war, unlike any of those before it, is not calling forth any 'religious' reaction? – what does that mean for 'Christianity'?' (2)

Z: That is a good question but does it make any sense to say there is Christianity without religion?

It certainly takes a while to get your head round it. Alan Jamieson has written a book called 'A Churchless Faith', note the title. (3) There are certainly many 'fresh expressions' of church. In Sheffield there is something called 'open mic' church which provides the opportunity for anyone to share anything they like. It has been described as 'Britain's Got Talent' without the judges, but with Jesus. There is also something gaining in popularity called 'Messy Church' in which families can sit around and take part in all kinds of activities.

Z: Messy Church sounds to be just up my street.

Pete Ward has written about 'liquid church'. (4)

Z: I wonder what kind of liquid. Would Alcoholics Anonymous approve?

That is not the point. This is liquid in the sense of being flexible and fluid. Liquid church is continually on the move, responding to the demands of the Gospel and the promptings of the Holy Spirit which like the wind 'blows where it chooses'. ( John 3: 8) Ward talks about church being a verb, not a noun, so we can say 'I church, you church, we church'. 'For too long we have seen church as something we attend.......If, however, the church is something that comes about when we make it, then walls come tumbling down. Suddenly being church and doing church become an exciting adventure.'(5) People today are talking about churches 'without walls'.

Z: You are stretching my imagination to think of a church without walls!

That's right. You are forced to look at the church in a completely different way.
You are not seeing different things but seeing things differently.

Z: Now that is very unlikely.

There is a poem by Stevie Smith in which she talks about drowning not waving. Someone is going through exactly the same physical motion but with a completely different intention. More importantly, they are perceived quite differently. How do we know what a person is doing until we make the effort to find out?

Z: I recall a story about a guy who met a young person who was wearing only one shoe. The guy said, 'I see you've lost your shoe young man'. The reply was, 'no, I've found one'.

That is a good example. The person is the same and he still has only one shoe but his answer completely changes our perception of him. What would happen if we looked at the church and saw it not as a cosy club where people, in the main, get along very nicely, but a group of people who are taking the demands of the gospel seriously.
It is significant to me that the Church grew before it had buildings, before it had a recognized ministry and before

it became the national religion when Constantine was the Roman Emperor way back in the fourth century.

Z: That may be so but you can't turn the clock back. You can only start from where you are not from where you would like to be. It reminds me of the joke about someone asking a farmer in Ireland how to get to a certain place. The farmer replied 'if you want to get there I wouldn't start from here'.

I know that only too well. I am convinced that there will always be people who want to gather round a table and celebrate the life, death, and resurrection of Jesus. Not only that, they want a place where they feel accepted and where their own story is listened to in a non-judgmental way. They want to explore the bible in the light of their own story and discover the impact it has on their own lives.

Z: Hang on a minute. You are talking about three different things there- the importance of story, the importance of other people, and the idea of being accepted. Can you take them one at a time?

1. Personal story is important because it cannot be questioned. It is not open to discussion as other statements are. Your personal experience, therefore, is of paramount importance and, of course, sharing with others may not only reinforce your story but also help you to make sense of it and put it into perspective. An additional advantage for a story is that they are an aid to the listener. A bonus is if the story teller or the listener can relate it to a biblical story or event.

The important thing about stories is that they have an innate power in that not only can they be easily remembered, but also, they can be interpreted at different levels. They are also very evocative. Who has not been moved when they have heard the words, Once upon a time…. or indeed heard the carol, Once in Royal David's city?

Z: This is nothing new is it? I thought Jesus told a few stories.

He certainly did. The problem is that over the years they have lost some of their potency. Let's take for example the parable of the Good Samaritan.

For the first hearers that was an incredibly powerful story because the Samaritans were thought of as little more than half breeds and heretics yet in the parable they are being used as an example of what it means to be a good neighbour. Even when we explain the background to the parable it is still difficult for present day readers to grasp the full impact of the story. Somehow we have to put the biblical stories into a modern idiom.

Z: I remember hearing about the parable of the good punk rocker.

Yes. It's that kind of idea but I don't pretend it is easy because even that is now out of date. Another thing to bear in mind is that if people have been attending church for years, they have heard the bible stories many times and it is very difficult for them to listen with any kind of freshness. In the same way, some of the images in the bible have lost their potency. For example, Jesus describes himself as the Bread of life. What if people no longer eat bread but prefer instead pasta, rice or oat cakes? Then some of the power of the imagery is lost. Jesus is no longer seen as the staff of life, or an essential ingredient of everyday life. In some countries Jesus is known as the coconut of life simply because the coconut comes from the coco palm, the tree of life.

Z: A different image would be Jesus as a clown – a symbol of joy, vulnerability, and hope.

Yes, and the clown is usually not a major act but comes on in between acts to relieve the tension. The clown is often a marginal figure but is, nevertheless, included in the community of the circus.

Z: I think you are going to talk about the church as community. What a surprise!

2. Who can argue that at its heart the Church is about community? To put it slightly differently, the church is about people. If there are no people, there is no church, only a building. Christianity is a faith which grew out of a group of people living in community, beginning with Jesus and the first disciples. My fear is that we have become locked into structures and organization and left out an essential element of Christianity, the idea of community. This is even sadder when one realises how much people are looking today for a sense of community.

However, it is not quite so simple. Organisation, for which principle John Wesley was renowned, and community tend to be incompatible. 'Committees and chair people do not a community make.' (6) Of course, some organisation is important otherwise anarchy takes over. 'But an organisation is able to nurture a measure of community within itself only to the extent that it is willing to risk or tolerate a certain lack of structure.' (7)

'Too often the church is a structure of tightly-orchestrated rules. The transcendent rarely goes by the rules. One has only to think of Jesus' entrance into this world to illustrate this. The entrance broke the accepted pattern. So did his exit, and his parables, and his life-style, and so on.' (8)

Z: Now you are in to my kind of world, but let me tell you, breaking the rules, is very risky. People can start to get very nervous and edgy. It is also very risky trying to get people to laugh. I feel such a fool if they don't. I feel an utter failure

Edison was trying to solve the problem of how to construct a filament for his brand- new electric light bulb. The task was to discover a filament that did not burn out. He had people working on the project for months. Finally the foreman of the work teams came to him, cap in hand, 'Mr. Edison, I am sorry to say we have done a thousand experiments and worked thousands of hours to find this filament and I am afraid to say it has all been for nothing'. Edison looked back at the man and said, "Nonsense, we know a thousand ways in which it doesn't work!'(9)

Failure was not seen as something negative but something very positive. Furthermore, only those who risk failure know how far they can go. Anyway, what is the alternative? 'If we try to avoid the risks, we will miss the possibilities.'(10) In any event, faith, by its very nature, is not the same as certainty and therefore involves risk.

Z: You can't learn to swim without getting in the water.

For some it is much easier to stay put, in the comfort zone. They have, to use your analogy Zeno, an inherent dislike or even fear of water. Indeed there are some who could be labelled traditionalists who are quite happy with the church. Moreover, the church is meeting their needs and so there is no need to change. To that extent they will continue to worship in traditional ways. Only time will tell how long this trend ill continue.

Z: Does God require museum keepers or pioneers?

Exactly. It is just very difficult taking a risk but without risk there is no growth. 'We are saved not by getting it right, but by the love that redeems us while we are getting it wrong.' (11) Some get very uncomfortable when there is the slightest change in the church. For example, removing the pews has provoked great anger and distress amongst more than a few.

Z: I thought pews were very uncomfortable. What is the problem? In any case it is very difficult to think of a community when people sit on hard pews all facing in one direction and there is very little eye contact with each other. In a circus the central focus is a ring around which people sit.

I agree. The irony is that even when pews are replaced by chairs they are very often placed in the same pattern. A person coming into church for the first time is faced with lines of 'backs' rather than welcoming faces. Imagine someone coming into your own home and receiving that kind of welcome. Body language communicates messages of various kinds, some of them unwittingly.

An idea being tried out in some places is Café church in which people sit round tables café style whilst worshiping. I came across this poem by Hilaire Kirkland

God and coffee

I went to a church and found there
      row upon row
of people facing one way
      like travellers in a railway carriage
listening to the word of God:
And the minister preached a splendid sermon,
and the robed choir sang their anthem,
and the solo voice flew like a thin reed wind
      over the stone people
         in wooden pews.

I went to a coffee bar and found there
      group upon group
of people huddled round tables
like conspirators in candlelight,
talking philosophy and religion:
And they sought God as only youth can,
and the brown coffee smouldered in the cups,
and the smoke smelt like incense
      in a new temple
         built for the Lord. (12)

Z: It certainly would be a new temple for the Lord!

3. An essential ingredient of community is acceptance. In other words, is the church a place where people can be themselves and thereby grow into what God wants them to be? (13) The New Testament offers us a vision of what human life could become. Paul in his letter to the Galatians says there are to be no divisions of any kind at all. As we have seen, Jesus goes out of his way to incorporate those who were deemed to be unacceptable – children, women, lepers, tax

gatherers and so on. Mark notes there was a Gentile, a non believer, at the foot of the cross. Matthew's star is seen from the whole universe and we are encouraged to go into all the world to talk about Jesus.

Z: My feeling is that the church has become a bit too tribal. It looks inward. What happened to you last Sunday?

Yes. I wandered into a church for a service, people smiled and I smiled back and afterwards I wandered out again. Nobody bothered to have a conversation and ask if I was visiting or on holiday and nobody bothered to ask me my name.

Z: You wouldn't normally let anybody come into your house without asking them their name. But are your points about story telling, community and acceptance enough? Is there anything else?

In his 'outline for a book' Bonhoeffer gives a radical direction the church needs to take. 'The Church is her true self only when she exists for humanity. As a fresh start she should give away all her endowments to the poor and needy. The clergy should live solely on the free will offering of their congregations, or possibly engage in some secular calling. She must take her part in the social life of the world, not lording it over men, but helping and serving them. She must tell men, whatever their calling what it means to live in Christ, to exist for others.' (14)

Z: That would create a stir.

It certainly would, but there is some truth in the argument. I have often felt going into a cathedral, for example, that it is a symbol of power and wealth when the thrust of the gospel is the complete opposite. I have never understood how the church managed to build some magnificent cathedrals in the midst of abject poverty. Today, the church, at least some churches, have untold wealth and yet there is so much need in the world. Bishops live in palaces and other clergy often live in very large rectories, vicarages or manses.

Z: How about the clergy living off free will offerings?

That is all very well but very difficult if one has a family to support. It is not much good going into the local supermarket saying you can't pay your bill because the congregation didn't like your sermon enough last week. However, the thought of secular work is very appealing. St. Paul, himself, was engaged in a tent making ministry. The signs are that we are moving in this direction, more by force of circumstances than by actual desire. Some churches can no longer afford full time clergy and so there is a movement towards local ministry, where people are engaged in secular work, or non stipendiary ministry. Christians are called to be servants and servants operate in other people's houses. They are also called to be salt and yeast.

Z: Neither of which are any use until they are put into something.

Precisely. Christians can be prone to escaping into their own little tribes or cliques and ignoring the demands of the world. I was struck recently by a big community event near where I live. Nowhere did I detect a Christian presence.

Z: Perhaps they were all secretly the leaven in the lump.

I would like to think so. Another example would be a

community event in one of my churches a few years ago. My appeal for volunteers met with a stony silence. Everybody was too busy – or maybe they didn't like the idea of being taken out of their comfort zone. In an age when we're in danger of 'amusing ourselves to death', we must ensure that we keep in touch with things that matter most.

Z: But I am in the job of amusing people.

I am not at all against people being amused. In fact, I am all for it. I like to watch a good programme on the television, or go to the cinema. If we are not careful, though, life can become very superficial and unsatisfying. All I am asking is that people keep asking questions. In particular, 'What really matters?' The church will never die so long as we keep asking questions about meaning and purpose.

Z: I sometimes wonder whether God is the question or the answer. I was wondering though what the effect would be if there were no churches at all? If the church at the end of your road suddenly disappeared would it be missed?

I think some people would certainly miss it at Christmas and Easter. There may well be changing patterns of church life in the future. Maybe Christians will meet in small groups and then meet as a large group two or three times a year for a long residential weekend together. If that were the case a building would no longer be necessary and therefore no longer would we need endless meetings and fund raising committees about maintaining a large church building. The church would be amongst the people acting as yeast or salt. The groups will probably be based around a table.

Z: I though food would come into it somewhere.

Yes, because as we have seen, food and hospitality were very important in the early church. Anyway, this is not just about church buildings and whether they are necessary or not. There is something much more profound going on. Writers from both ends of the theological spectrum talk about the church being in exile. Whitworth comes from the conservative evangelical strand of Christianity and he has written a book called 'Prepare for exile, a new spirituality and mission for the church'. (15) Spong, on the other hand, comes from a radical tradition and has written a book entitled, 'Why Christianity must change or die, a bishop speaks to believers in exile'. (16)

Z: I'm not sure I fancy that idea.

Like it or not it is happening. The feeling first occurred to me over 20 years ago when, for some reason that I can't remember, I found myself in a shopping centre on Good Friday. I felt completely alienated and out of place. This was a culture I felt I didn't belong to and mentally, let alone spiritually, I was in a completely different place. I just had to go home. I get similar feelings on a Sunday morning when the majority of the population are in the local supermarket, or the local car boot sale, or on the playing fields, or the garden centre or visiting family, and so on and so on. There is a plethora of alternatives to going to church on a Sunday morning.

Z: Maybe some just lie in bed after a night out on Saturday.

I guess so. Another thing. Whatever happened to Pentecost?

Z: I can't imagine.

Whitworth writes, 'to be an exile is essentially to be forced out of your homeland, to become a stranger in a foreign land'. (17) Spong writes, 'exile is never a voluntary experience, it is always something forced upon a person or a people by things or circumstances over which the affected ones have no control'. (18) Of course, the experience of exile is not new. In the Old Testament much of the story is about the experience of exile and both Whitworth and Spong write about this aspect of our spiritual heritage.

Whereas Whitworth feels an alienation with the culture and says, 'we must see the gap which is opening up ever more between our culture, the state and the church and the sense of exile that is bringing' ,(20) Spong is more concerned with the alienation between himself and a typical Christian believer. 'I live in a state of exile from the presuppositions of my own religious past.............I am a believer who increasingly lives in exile from the traditional way in which Christianity has heretofore been proclaimed.'(21) He goes on to say that 'the hunger for God is deep and pervasive in our society today. We need to recognize that this is not the same thing as hunger for the answers the church has traditionally given. Indeed, many seekers today do not act as if the Church will ever be a place where God can be fruitfully sought'. (21)

I have written about both these aspects of alienation. For me both the culture and the church are speaking in a language I find difficult to understand. The question is, how much do I conform to the culture and simply go along with the prevailing trends. It is one thing to try to understand a culture but it is quite another to conform to it.

Z: Somehow I see you more as a non-conformist.

I hope so. Part of the gospel is to act counter culturally. Paul says 'do not be conformed to this world, but be transformed by the renewing of your minds, so that you may discern what is the will of God'. (Roms. 12:2) The other problem for me is trying to translate traditional church language into a form that is meaningful today. As soon as one becomes disenchanted with the kind of God in the sky who dispenses punishments to those who are bad and rewards to those who are good then what replaces it? If a Father Christmas idea of God no longer fits the bill then what does?

Z: It seems to be quite a tricky place living in exile.

Tricky is not quite the word. Certainly, I sometimes feel out of place and therefore quite vulnerable. There is also hope and excitement that the church will re-form itself and become much more meaningful to more people. I feel strongly that Christianity will undoubtedly survive. For example, in China, where the church was almost extinguished under Chairman Mao, it has begun to grow again. In one sense, the church will only continue to live so long as it is prepared to keep on dying.

Z: Maybe some people are unnecessarily anxious about the future. Temples, coliseums, castles, palaces, cathedrals, even civilisations will decay and fall, of that there is no doubt. What will remain are those who are 'foolish' enough to gather round a table and remember the story of Jesus.

I think you have a point Zeno. Paul himself says that not even the future will separate us from the love of God. God will be there to meet and greet us in the future. Paul also wonders whether people are 'foolish' enough to believe.

Z: I, for one, certainly am.

# Points to Ponder:

1. What kind of body language does your church or group project?

2. What message do people pick up from looking at your church or community building?

3. If things continue as they are where do you foresee your church will be in ten years time?

4. How does your church enable the sharing of personal stories?

5. In what ways do you feel alienated from society?

# Meditation:

Become aware of your body – your feet on the ground, your bottom on the chair, the feel of your clothes on your shoulder, any aches and pains............ This brings you into the here and now and that is where God is. The past has happened and can't be changed, the future is not yet, the present is all we have.

# References

1. Bonhoeffer, op. cit. p.91
2. ibid.
3. Jamieson, Alan, <u>A churchless Faith,</u> SPCK, 2003
4. Ward, Pete, <u>Liquid Church</u>, Paternoster, 2003

5.  ibid. p.3
6.  Peck, Scott M., The Different Drum, Arrow, 1990, p.93
7.  ibid.
8.  Leibenow, Mark, Is there fun after Paul? Resource Publications, Inc. 1987, p.45
9.  Whyte, David, The Heart Aroused, Doubleday, 1994, p.95
10. Runcorn, David, Choice, Desire, and the Will of God, SPCK, 2003, p.34
11. Holloway, op. cit., p.181
12. Hilaire Kirkland, source to be checked
13. see 'All are welcome' a hymn in Common Ground, Saint Andrew Press, Edinburgh, 2008
14. Quoted in Honest to God, p.135
15. Whitworth, Patrick, Prepare for Exile, SPCK, 2008
16. Spong, John Shelby, Why Christianity must change or die, Harper Collins, 1999
17. Whitworth, op. cit. p.xiv
18. Spong, op. cit., p.22
19. Whitworth, op. cit., p.33
20. Spong, op. cit., p.20
21. ibid., p.21

Lightning Source UK Ltd.
Milton Keynes UK
UKOW040701111112

201981UK00001B/3/P